Spotlight Poets

Daydream Believer

Edited by Chiara Cervasio

Spotlight Poets

First published in Great Britain in 2004 by
SPOTLIGHT POETS
Remus House
Coltsfoot Drive
Peterborough
PE2 9JX
Telephone: 01733 898102
Fax: 01733 313524
Website: www.forwardpress.co.uk

SB ISBN 1 84077 105 4

Foreword

As a nation of poetry writers and lovers, many of us are still surprisingly reluctant to go out and actually buy the books we cherish so much. Often when searching out the work of newer and less known authors it becomes a near impossible mission to track down the sort of books you require. In an effort to break away from the endless clutter of seemingly unrelated poems from authors we know nothing or little about; Spotlight Poets has opened up a doorway to something quite special.

Daydream Believer is a collection of poems to be cherished forever; featuring the work of eleven captivating poets each with a selection of their very best work. Placing that alongside their own personal profile gives a complete feel for the way each author works, allowing for a clearer idea of the true feelings and reasoning behind the poems.

The poems and poets have been chosen and presented in a complementary anthology that offers a variety of ideals and ideas, capable of moving the heart, mind and soul of the reader.

Chiara Cervasio

Contents

The Authors
& Poems

Donna Louise Salisbury

My name is Donna Louise Salisbury and I'm twenty-three. I'm a housewife and I have a wonderful husband, two adorable boys and a cute and cuddly Staff called Bella. I have lived in the Rhondda Valleys all my life, and am now settled in a little town called Penygraig.

I have always loved reading and writing for as long as I can remember. I used to love writing poetry and stories when I was at school, and I was always fascinated with the music on 'Murder She Wrote'.

I think that's when I decided that I wanted to be a writer, be it poetry or stories. My inspirations as I was growing up were the wonderful Charles Dickens, Kenneth Grahame and my all time favourite Roald Dahl. I've read tons of wonderful stories through the years, but the above three authors always come out on top. These days I read a wide range of modern poetry magazines as well as Stephen King and Danielle Steel. I think J K Rowling is one of the best children's authors of today. She's helped children want to read books again, as well as us adults.

I've only started writing poetry seriously in the last eighteen months, but I feel I've had a good response to my work. I've had poems published in my local papers, as well as poetry magazines and books. I am proud of what I have achieved and I feel that my work has gone from strength to strength.

I love to write about my perceptions of life, love and nature. My inspirations vary, sometimes it can be something someone has said, or something I have read. Other times I get inspired by a sunny day or a walk in the park. But my favourite type of poetry is the type that deals with emotions like love, anger, hurt etc. Things we all have to deal with, every day of our lives.

Ode To Flu

Lock me in a padded cell,
where it's warm and clean.
Just give me a box of tissues
and a nice warm jet of steam.
My eyes they are all watery,
my nose it's gone all red.
I haven't got the energy
to leave this ruddy bed.
My body is all shaky,
my cheeks are totally pale,
my tongue is like a boulder,
in a mouth that is so stale.
Don't hug me or kiss me,
I'm all full of germs,
the sweat is just pouring,
my whole body is one big ache.
This flu is one problem
I can't seem to shake.
When will this be over?
Not for a week or two,
someone get me the doctor,
so I can feel as good as new.
Next time I'm gonna be prepared,
hot water bottles and the like.
I don't want to feel like this again,
on these long, cold winter nights.

Remember Youth

Here's to our youth
The days we spent in the sun.
Those special days out,
With a close loved one.
Those days on the beaches,
Where our spirits ran free.
To the days in front of the fire,
Or singing around the Christmas tree.
Remember kicking a ball?
Or just dressing a doll?
Just sitting around talking?
Watching the leaves fall?
Our youth is so precious,
We should cherish it well.
Because before we know it
We're all grown up
Life is full of problems and mistrust
So keep youth in your heart
And your memories near,
And you'll always be young
No matter how old you are.

Wounded Souls, Healing Hearts

My heart has been broken and shattered,
But has been put back piece by piece.
For I have found an understanding of great depth,
And an even deeper sense of peace.
The logic of love is a complex thing,
The heart's reason is unknown.
It is soft and adoring,
But like a scorpion, a sting in its tail.
Jealousy the green-eyed monster,
Master of emotions,
Spears us when we least expect it,
And shatters all our dreams.
But with a little bit of magic,
From another wounded soul,
A broken heart is mended,
'And this I know'.

Affinity

I have found a love,
As rich as a pharaoh's tomb.
I feel just like a butterfly,
Emerging from its cocoon.
I feel bold,
I feel young,
There is a song of joy in my heart.

You're my charm of protection,
When danger is near.
You soothe away all thoughts of fear.
I cannot breathe,
I cannot think,
My mind is in overload.

We've risked a lot to get this far,
Our hearts sought each other out.
A multicoloured destiny,
Our paths of life marked out.
Together forever,
You and I,
My one and only sweet ally.

Believe

I believe in miracles,
I believe they come true.
Like when the angels of the heavens,
Guided me to you.

I believe in spirit,
Upon their astral cloud.
I believe the things I've done,
Have often made them proud.

I believe that dreams come true,
When you make a wish so sweet.
I believe that when times are bad,
We all deserve a treat.

I believe there's more to life,
Than being born and growing old.
I believe there's something out there,
Waiting to unfold.

I believe in my children,
Whom I love with all my heart.
I believe that no matter where we are,
We are never far apart.

Love's Crusades

Days of eternity,
Who'll count them for me?
Lord of love, let it be you,
Upon your throne of grace.
Help this stony heard bleed emotion,
Help the salty tears to flow,
Untangle my emotions
With your fire-tipped golden dart,
Pierce it deep within,
This cold-pressed, stony heart.

Awaken my senses to new love,
Be the knight at my side.
Let us be two bodies
Joined in one soul,
My personal elixir of life.
Be my mighty warrior,
Crusading for all that's good,
Showing me all the right things,
A knight of valour should.

Lullaby

As I cradle you sweet baby,
I give you all my love.
As the angels of the heavens
Sprinkle their sleeping dust.
I'll protect you,
Till morning comes,
You've nothing to fear my love.
So close your eyes sweet baby,
You have your mother's love.

As you dream your angel dreams
And you smile at what you see.
I'm still holding you sweet baby,
Cradled upon my knee.

Friends Forever

We've known each other for so long now,
Friends for so many years.
We've come so far and done so much,
Been together through thick and thin.
A bond was formed the day we met
A friendship of love and understanding,
Other friends have come and gone
But we've still stuck together.
So many adventures, so much fun we've had,
Our deepest secrets we have shared.
This friendship is forever,
You're my best friend
A shoulder I can lean on,
When I feel there's no light ahead.
I would do the same for you,
That's what friends are for,
My door is always open
No matter what the hour.
Just one more thing I have to say,
It's important that you know.
Dear sister held within my heart,
I'm glad that you chose me.

Childhood Recollections

Those childhood days
Full of adventure,
Explorers in pursuit of our dreams.
Every day as exciting as the one before.
Always together,
Hiding, seeking,
Finding treasures of old.
Climbing trees, ghost hunting,
Being scared, being bold.

A friendship, a bond,
From Heaven it was sent.
Creating mischief and laughter,
Wherever we went.
Having picnics, going swimming,
Doing projects together.
Listening to music, reading books,
Together whatever the weather.

Childhood recollections
Swirl in my heart,
From years of fabulous fun.
A stitch in time,
That is alone mine.
My special cloak of happiness.

Soulmates Forever

We're soulmates
Brought back together,
It was our time to meet again.
Shuffled and reborn,
But in a different guise.
Passed through centuries of time,
We've lived and loved in other lives.
We're an unbreakable part of each other,
We think and move as one.
My first love,
My last love,
I'm bound and chained to you.
My personal shaft of sunlight,
You're the heart,
In the ocean of my mind.
These words of wisdom for you and me,
'A love that risks nothing is worth nothing'.
I love you.

Daddy

To the very best daddy that I know,
The one they love and treasure,
Your laughter, your smile,
Your sparkly eyes,
You make all their days a pleasure.

Patience vast and loyalty true,
A heart bigger than the heavens,
A wonderful man,
Who lights up their lives
And to whom they will always turn.

Your loving hand and wisdom,
Has made these children strong and brave,
A father who lights up their lives
And makes sure they're always safe.

How lucky you are my darlings,
To have him for your daddy.

Gone

Summer has gone,
It eloped with the spring
Autumn and winter descend,
Like a queen and a king
And their son, Jack Frost,
With his friends storm and wind
Cause chaos once more,
It's their special thing.
Snow hasn't decided yet,
If she will come,
But if she does
It'll be freak and fun.

It's time for the parties,
Masks, fire and celebrations,
A witch's delight
Casting spells and revelations.

A new year lies ahead,
Time for new resolutions
To tell the truth
Of the spirits domain
That we all live on
And will come back again.

Nature's Victory

Golden rays of an autumn dawn
Caress me as I look
Upon the regal, golden carpet
Under my unworthy feet.
Nature's green is changing
Into a sea of wondrous colours.
Naked branches stare down
At their gleaming leaves,
Conversing in hushed tones.
The sweet song of a feathered friend,
An overwhelming sense of calm.
Glowing cheeks,
My nose is red,
As the wind whistles all around.
At this moment,
I could be the only one on Earth,
But the buzz of life is not far away.
So much beauty,
So much peace.
I feel proud to see
The richness of the changing year.
Another victory for Mother Nature,
She is supreme.

To Spring

As winter bids a sad farewell
And spring arrives with grace,
Dewdrops glisten like crystal shards,
Upon lush grass that resembles lace.
Birdsong echoes in every tree,
A song of new life heavy in the air.
Flowers bloom under clear blue skies,
They open with power and flare.
Fresh tended fields show a farmer's love,
For his way of life.
Winter's gone and spring is here,
The season that he loves.

Laura Perkins

Hi I'm Laura Perkins, I'm 17 and studying for my A levels at King Alfred's Community and Sports College in Wantage, where I also help out as a sports assistant. I'm hoping to go on to become a PE teacher.

I've been writing poetry since I was 14 and have had 16 poems published in three years. I wrote my first poem when I lost someone close to me and the most recent one to be accepted for publication is a thank you poem for three close friends of mine. I didn't know how to thank them enough for their friendship so writing a poem seemed the best idea.

Different things going on around inspire me to write poems. I've had two published on bullying, because it happened to me once and I hate to see others suffer as I did. The first poem was to let the bullies know how it really feels to be tormented and called names. The second one asked the bullies why they don't listen to people.

My poems cover a wide variety of topics, as it's always a new theme every time I write one.

I like writing poetry as it gives me a chance to express my feelings. When writing a new poem I find it easier to write if it's something that's happened to me, that way it all comes from the heart.

Thank You

(To Chris, Sue and Caroline
This one is for you; it really helped having you around.
Thanks for everything you've done for me)

Thank you for making time to chat about my troubles,
Thank you for helping me when I was worried,
Thank you for giving advice when I was down,
Thanks for being a mate and just being around,
Thank you for keeping me positive,
Thanks for understanding,
Thanks for putting up with me when I was having a bad day,
It means a lot to me,
To have mates like you,
I can't say thank you enough.

Bullied

This is how you feel when you're bullied:
You get a niggly feeling inside,
Your puffy red eyes hurt when you've cried,
You wipe away the tears; you're trying to hide,
You feel that all your hopes have died,
You sob while your bully's glowing with pride.

This is how you feel when you're bullied:
You don't feel the same,
You imagine you're to blame,
They shout at you and call you names,
As your happiness burns away like wood to a flame.

This is how it feels when you're bullied:
You just want to die,
You curl up on your bed when you lie,
Your mum hugs you as you cry and cry, to smiles and laughs
You say goodbye.

This is how it feels when you're bullied
At night say a prayer
Never bully as a dare.

Listen To Me

I try to run and hide from you,
But you find me no matter what I do,
You tease and taunt when it's me you want,
Why won't you leave me alone?
I cry all night,
When you're not in sight,
You just can't see,
What you're doing to me,
It doesn't show on the outside,
But if you look inside,
You'd see I was heartbroken,
Why won't you leave me alone?
Won't you listen?
Can't you see?
You're a bully and you're picking on me.

Remember Me

Remember me,
With my wicked laugh,
And funny sense of humour,
There was always a huge grin,
On my fave,
I'll always be a smiler you said,
Those spikes on my head,
That you all loved,
And how I do it,
Still remains a secret
I'd laugh at anything,
You know me.
One giggle
Ended in a huge laugh.
Always getting in trouble,
Because the laugh went too far,
I hope that's the way
You'll remember me.
I don't think I need to give a name,
With the details I give,
You'll know straight away,
That it's your mate.

In With The New

First time in years
Amazing
I was suddenly being congratulated
What had I done
That people liked
All those years
I went through with people having a go
I could never do anything right
Then just like that people were helping me out
I think I like it like this
The old me has gone
And the new me is ready for a challenge
I've only just realised myself that I've changed
I tackle things instead of them tackling me
I'm going to stay like this now
'Cause after seeing life in a different light
I've figured out that things are worth a go
And I'm not going to give up
Life really does have a good side
And I think I've finally found it.

Sisters

Sisters who need them,
Some people hate their sisters and never want to see them again,
But me, I love mine.
And enjoy spending each and every day with her,
We argue and fight like other sisters,
But we have a bond that puts things right
I like being the oldest,
As I'm there if she's in trouble,
Or ever needs help.
She'll do the same for me one day,
At the minute she's too young to understand,
I'll always stand by her whatever she's done,
I'm here like a friend or a best mate,
If she ever needs a shoulder to cry on.
So one day I'll pray and hope that she will do the same
So in a way we're not just sisters,
We're mates as well.
She's my only sister,
I think that's why I love her so much,
It's just her and me.

What Did I Do?

What did I do?
To desire this
Stress and agro
If I had one single wish
I'd go back to start again
And tell you it was wrong
Why won't you listen?
Can't you see?
There's going to be trouble
And grief
And you'll be in the middle
You always are
And always will be.
You think you're hard
But the things you do
Are stupid and silly
But will you listen?
No.
You need to stop fooling yourself
You're not as hard as you look
Just remember that next time
When you do something like you did
Ask yourself
'Why me?
Why was I there'
Then perhaps you'll remember that breaking up your family
Isn't worth it just to act hard and look cool.
That's all I want to know
What have I done to you?
To go through this now and feel as guilty as you.

Spotlight Poets

The Dark

I feared the dark as a child
And if I had to go upstairs alone
I'd make sure all the lights were on first
If a shadow came wondering past
I'd jump out of my skin and scream
Whatever it may be
I'd fear there would be something hiding
Among my bed sheets,
Under the bed,
Or even behind the curtain
I never have been one for the dark
And I still fear it at seventeen.

Dedicated To . . . Mum

I'm sorry for all the things I've said and done
I know I can't change the past
But we should look into the future
And forget the past
I want you to know
That some day
I'll be your perfect girl
The one that's always loved you
The touch of your love
Will heal me
My only wish is for you to see
That I love you no matter what
I've loads of thank yous
But I think you already know that
You've always been there for me
And got me out of trouble
So this isn't just to say sorry
It's a big thank you as well
Some day I'll be a well known name
For what I do not for what I've done
And I'll have you to thank.

Heaven

What is Heaven?
Where is Heaven?
Nobody knows.
Is it a place where nice people go?
I hope so.
I'd like to know the answers to these,
So I know that my loved ones are there,
In my mind
Heaven's like a dream, waiting to come real.
White fluffy clouds and bright stars,
So really Heaven needs an answer,
I'd like to know if my nan was up there,
God, where are you when people need answers?
All I can do is wish.

Hope

I found hope the other day,
In the stars up in the dark night's sky,
And the mountains way up high,
The oceans seemed so far away,
But the rain kept falling,
And the days kept moving,
In the dark the stars would be my guide,
To me life becomes a different meaning,
Where you could look at the rainbows,
And count the colours,
Sounds like a dream, doesn't it?
The days I had were special,
Still I was young then and eager,
But things haven't really changed,
Because I still like to dream these games.

Nan

It's only just really hit me
That I've nobody to talk to
And
Share things with
All I'm left with is pictures to talk to
I wish you were here Nan, I really do
I still think of you
I wonder where you are and what you're doing
I hope you're safe
Nan, my only wish is for you to see
How much I still love you
My heart still hurts inside
I keep hoping you'll come back
I'll love you forever
Stay safe Nan.

SpotLight Poets

Neil Campbell Roper

 Neil Campbell Roper is an experienced freelance journalist and short story writer. After giving poetry readings at Pentameters, in its early days, Neil has been extensively published in various anthologies and literary reviews as much in France as in the UK. He writes equally in French and English and his poetry has been translated into French. While in WA he wrote and directed a play, also two other plays were given a rehearsed reading.

He furthermore featured with the Australian Broadcasting Corporation, in the poetry programme *In Tempo*, where he read his own work.

He has translated and adapted into English five books from French and Italian, including the latest publication, from Russian, entitled *Childhood* by the renowned Vadim Andreyev. Neil has extensively translated the work of Janine Fuchs and Luce Peclard, contemporary Swiss French poets. A major project is to translate into book form the work of the recently deceased Genevan poet, Luc Vuagnat, whose work has individually appeared in English in many literary reviews including the *London Magazine*.

Literary awards, prizes and distinctions conferred on Neil were the *Grand Prix d'Edition, Belgium;* the *Diploma de Benemerenza, Roma;* the *Certificate of Merit (International Who's Who in Poetry, CUP);* all were for poetry. He was a poetry prize-winner in the Alexander Searle Literary Association's competition, 2001.

Lighthouse

In the midst of storm seas
Born from clusters of rocks
I rise tall and white
Scanning the far horizons
Of darkened ocean
Alone amidst hurricanes and typhoons
I watch over the world
Through day and night
So the ships of mankind
Pass safe with my light
I am outpost of the land
Outsider in oceans
Bearing in my stone heart
Secrets of the future

The Call Of Queen Hatshepsut

Over the velvet void
Of darkness
Clothing the Nile
Sightless
Save three white masts
Felucca* swaying
Along the bank
Soundless
Golden aura of light
In the distance
Across sugar cane fields
Over date palms
The regal three-tiered crown
In limestone and granite
Your reign lives on
To this day
Queen of splendour and art

(* Nile boat with tall sails)

Stranger

Stranger
Tell me
If eyes are mirrors of desire
Tell me
If lips are doors of healing
Tell me
If hands are flowers of feeling

Stranger
Tell me
The course to wisdom
Tell me
The path to beauty
Tell me
The way to truth

Stranger
Tell me
If hours are halls of hope
Tell me
If days are threads of joy
Tell me
That life is master of all

Day Of Mourning

Though all the days and weeks before
Your face had smiled
As warm and lovely as the sun
Which strolled across
Sicilian skies . . .
That day you cried

Tears were streaming from your eyes
Your body shook with grief
The sun itself seemed lost to sight
And yet the day was bright
That day you cried

You would not say a word
But pointed to the garden
Where almond and acacia trees
Breathed summer's ease
That day you cried

Amidst the jasmine flowers
A truck a hideous symbol stood
Some workmen idling
Cement lay piled against the terrace wall
That day you cried

A cypress tree though sacred
As the centuries which had watched
It grow: green flame of grace
Lay dead across the garden path
That day you cried

Truck roared to life
Gears growled angrily
The workmen nursed it past
The naked stump
Then I knew why
That day you cried

Life

Being of my life
Life of my being
Light in my darkness
Darkness in light
Star in my night
Comet of laughter
Speed for my slowness
You slow down to smile
Ineffable love
In your eyes

Spotlight Poets

Recollection

Shall I remember you when time has fled
From present passion's violent fusions?
When colours of your humours finely wed
Are formed into a rainbow of illusions?

Or shall I, having felt the embers of your heart,
Reflect that, after all, your love grew like a flower,
In bloom among the past before being part
Of treasured relics like a transient hour.

Or else? What more could I desire,
Than to pursue with weary but yet steady will
The phantom of your smile, your lips that flamed a fire
Devoured my thoughts, where cinders flicker still?

Spring

How little yet man understands:
Life is a ceaseless stream
That's flowing through his hands,
In vain he tries to hold the surging waves,
To realise the transient dream
Confused in life's commotion,
Until the water merges fast
Into the boundless ocean.

In Praise Of Youth

('She walks in beauty like the night of cloudless climes and starry skies
And all that's best of dark and bright meets in her aspect and her eyes.'
Lord Byron)

Into the room I strode and thought another round
Of faces blank and dull once more I'd found
Not so from out the grey parade
There gleamed a light so great it banished shade
Another sun was born from cloudless skies
With cosmic heat pulsating from her eyes
More black than brown but growing to a smile
That haunts me still with candour lack of guile
She swayed a carnal flower among the dead
Such fragrance in her breath overwhelmed my head
Her hair stacked high a sheen of black
I pictured undulating down her back
Speak could I not From lips as petalled red
Flowed words I barely heard
So fine her features they killed the mind
My being became as one turned blind
Long has she gone, not ever to return
Through languid hours I'm left to yearn
The kiss she never gave
Her perfume haunts me now and to the grave

The Sun

Blinking awake with golden eyes
Each morning I arise
Above the seas and continents
To spread my silver arms
Across the skies
All earth within my warm embrace
Knows not the emptiness of space
But circles round my burning face
One half bright the other night
Seeking still my omnipresent
Light

Sea

Becalmed I blush at the cool kiss of light
Watch soundless the sun's flight as he soars
Quivering with orange wings across the east
I hold the skies' complexion in my arms
Gleam with myriad smiles in many hours
I whisper to myself with lips that barely stir
My glittering dress unfolds in midday heat
To shores where man is monarch
On my back I bear his craft safe today
But often in ire wed to the wind
I arch up my spine in columns of spray
Toss them like toys in my waves' laughter
Where they smash and dissolve
With the ill-gotten gains of greed
Forever in silence I nurture
On my bed these relics of grandeur and pageantry
So beloved by man
With evening I change tune to wear crimson and gold
Restless I cast myself in curling white tongues
On golden sands timelessly breathing
The rhythm of centuries
Herald of life and destruction
Married to sunlight
Hounded by winds
I move without ceasing
Yet never move

Man And The Computer

Humans
Peripatetic digits
Filed and stored
In intergalactic computers
By self-propagating bureaucrats
Silently playing
With nameless numbers
Made dots and signs
Flashing lights
Pushing knobs
For electronic hymns
To the formless god
Of uniformity
The night-long chanting
Of memory disks
Massed in towers
Of concrete and glass
Waiting to be tapped
No big brother's above us
Only the faceless spectre
Of one-dimensional
Man

Man And The Media

From the brash new world
Of seductive supershelves
Of swanky supermarkets
Daily shrines to worship
At the altar of consumerism
Rush home to the evening tide
Of soaps and mini-soaps
Recline in the bottomless well
Of armchair leisure
Stabbed by daggers of ads
Playground of gadgets
Possessions that possess
Mirage of instant success
Battle of sights and sounds
In your brains bombarded
By missiles of sibilant slogans
Sinking to survive
In worn-out clichés
Chewing the cud of constant pictures
Assailed from all sides
By radios records and disks
But tele's a friend
Pandora's box to soothe and provoke
Jungle of jingles
Unending flow
Till death us do part

Planet Earth

From time unknown
I circle round
In wedding to the sun

Cradle of mankind
Womb of the world
I gave birth to continents
Islands and rivers

Century after century
You plundered my soils
You hacked down my forests
You sullied my streams
You dirtied my oceans

Man you were given a garden
You made it a junkyard

Soon I'll burst out in rage
With tremors and quakes
I cannot take in anymore
The dross of your modern mistakes
The bombs that you blast in my belly
Will be wounds in the flank of the future
Man you will know my real nature

Snow Scene

(In memory of Switzerland)

White language of the skies
Which speak in silent monologues
On mountains scarved with mist
Where firs alone stand mournful watch
To days that have no end
And no beginning
When peaks are pregnant with disaster

White language of the skies
Which deaden human will
On roadways lined with drifts
Where cars abandoned hold no hope
To days that have no dawn
And no unfolding
When peaks are pregnant with disaster

Homage To The Penan

We move at ease
Beneath a canopy of trellised trees
Our roof
We live at peace
Beside the soaring trunks of wood
Our walls
We watch in awe
Among the rainbow wings of birds
Our songs
We track each day
Blowpipe in hand our forest game
Our strength

One day we woke
Incredulous with dread
To hear the growl and whine
Of dozers saws around us
The slow and searing crack
Of living trees being felled

All day and night we hear machines
We see the trunks lying dead across our floor
Our walls are crumbling in
Our roof's become the sky
The water of our streams brings death
The prey we used to hunt: extinct

We cannot understand why every day
We have less land
Invaded by a foreign hand
We are now the forest game
Staked out for stately profit

Philip Naylor

I am 16 years of age and am rather new to the world of poetry. I have had poems published with Forward Press, Dogma Publications, Cyberwit and Reflections. Every poem I write holds a certain depth and meaning, even if not instantly seen.

I am currently living in Liverpool, where I was born, and have no view of leaving. I like the city, the people and the general feel deduced from just being here. I would challenge those who still hold stereotypical views of this city to remove their prejudicial and out-dated opinions, and search for fact rather than believing the bias views of media, and the harmful and very rarely truthful tales that stem from gossip.

My background I suppose would be described as an 'unstable' one, I am not happy with everything that has affected and in some instances, still is affecting my life, but then that is what makes up me, and who I am at the present moment in time. I believe everything happens for a reason, and that the things in my life that are less desirable are blessings in disguise, as they allow me to draw on actual experience, rather than imagination. I am hoping for a successful career in poetry, as well as a broad one.

Betrayal

You are blind, and always will be,
Toward my being.
You cannot see what I will do next,
Will I slay your soul, betray you?
And if so, how can you protect?
Yes, love is blind but so is life,
'You can never truly know someone'.
You can never place that much trust,
Merely on word of mouth.
But we must . . . mustn't we?
For if we don't, and God forbid, everyone should turn their back
On the world, then what a lifeless sordid place.
So we walk about with our three quarter length facades
Speaking of how we all have it hard,
Waiting for the exposure of a nice clean back,
And for our own preservation, we instinctively attack.

Bloodstained Hands

The light would lick my face, hanging from the lightbulb
like a spider from a web. Gently connecting with my skin
illuminating my discomfort as I sat in my room,
alone, again.
Living in my memories, watching that screen in my head
as it played my life back in short twenty second clips.
Eyes turning from pink to red as a brave lone tear
journeys to my lips.
Slamming the door on reality I can hide,
in constant darkness my mind can subside,
for who would want to love a person who cannot love themselves?
A draft inside me, something keeps rubbing against my organs,
you know the feeling. Just not quite right.
Pulling back I can see myself murdered on the floor,
my heart torn,
what bothers me most when adjusting my sight,
is I am the owner of the bloodstained hands.

Cold Heart

In a cold, dormant corner of my heart I sit,
next to me sits someone, who isn't there.
Who hasn't been for quite some time,
in a heart of mine, I sit, alone.
From the unsolid walls, echoes
the sound of crying . . . years of it.
The oppression leaks from all corners . . .
the tears have come and gone . . .
and come again . . . but no more do they flood
from the crimson corners of my eyes.
My heart bled, but bleeds no more,
for I am empty at the core.
I hold no centre, none at all . . .
a mere stony shell.
My heart wraps itself in shadows,
fictitious love.
The space where it should have been set,
remains untouched.
Alcatraz. The secret garden,
from such bad luck,
I pray your pardon.

Cyber Hell

I sit, entranced by this screen,
this cyber-hell.
That demands my attention,
and my thoughts as well.
No time to feel the drops of love,
that fall forever, to my heart's pool.
Such a fool, for sacrificing a life,
and admitting it. For erasing all my hard work,
and submitting it.
For passing myself in thought,
and forgiving it.
But most of all, for owning a life, and not living it.

Encrypted

I'm falling again,
slipped on the edge, wet feet against the stone.
Shooting past all things that tried to push me,
the troubled clouds and teasing branches.
Alone, dropped by the hands of God,
litter to the bin.
The flames dancing inside me, tearing at my skin.
Not stopping at the death of all things me,
not content until they have devoured all.
My soul and being a pile of ash,
an exhibition inside a human shell.
People staring and pointing, looking at their guides for
my description.
No need to destroy me,
I was simply encrypted.

Fire In The Trees

The air outside, an invisible blanket of ice
that lays against the skin with hidden pins.
That momentary shock as face collides with glass
and paralysis for a moment grabs your limbs.
When looking out the window to the garden,
to the glass the brickwork and the green.
I see what can only be described as a natural wonder,
I see the fire in the trees.
The brown and rotting leaves, laying edged from the branches,
I see the skeleton exposed, as the rays set the body alight.
Enhancing its beauty as it stands still above the houses,
peaceful, awaiting the night.

How You Had To Learn

Comforted by the darkness that wraps you,
allowing your eyes to be seduced by the radiant picture,
the highlighted reminder.
You scan the rugged edges, the mark of time,
swipe your finger across the dust-kissed face.
Replaying the rolls and rolls of tape,
stored in your memory.
Their smile, and scent, the way they walked,
You're bent on breaking the laws of the universe
and taring through dimensions.
The connection of skin, two hands, embracing each other
for one final time.
This time knowing it's the last.
Instead of all those days that passed,
complacent with the little things you had,
sad that this is how you had to learn . . .

I Always Listen

I listen, two open windows to the world,
mounted on my head. Never closed.
As they speak to me, intertwined within the wind,
blowing the net curtains, as they dance in the night.
I listen as they tell me how they cried,
how their day has been one catastrophe after another.
How at work they messed up, and were fired,
and were cheated on by their lover.
I listen as the news streams on at six.
To the world I listen, to the wars and the people,
to the issues.
To the man preaching on the pavement, of the prophets,
I listen to them all.
I listen to the traffic on the roads, to the birds when they sing,
to the sirens of a night, as they pierce the air.
I always listen.
But speak, I don't dare.

I Am Determined

I have not been awarded 'best' in this subject,
does that detract from my skill?
If I write, and words are born in perfect form,
should I continue struggling still?
The sweat that forces itself from sandpaper skin
when thought is driving overtime.
Eyes staring on from behind, gritted eyelashes,
thinking they are teeth.
Clashing against one another with so much frustration
blood is called upon to surface.
'Everyone needs that pat on the back'
An eruption beneath the skin I am sure is in
occurrence. A shy smoke filters through the pores,
like burgling forces, removing all your thoughts.
The weed and the flower, one a talented beauty,
from nature has risen. The other, intrusive, life sucking,
living. With my hardened blood if required, I shall pave the way,
and every time they block the path, I'll start a-new,
with scars and wounds that litter my flesh, from angry hands
and dangerous tongues. I shall sink my flag into this world,
into this 'Elite', for I am determined.

I Don't Want To Talk About It

I don't want to talk about it,
replaying how you decorated my soul
only to put it on the property market,
an abandoned wreck.
I don't want to talk about it,
how you scarred my heart,
tore apart my insides
and simply walked away.
I don't want to talk about it,
I hate you, but I love you,
a bitter sweet comparison,
that's why there's so many clashes.
I don't want to talk about it,
how at night I'd lie awake and think,
tears playing on my face.
Verging on the brink of insanity.
Laying near lifeless alone in the dark,
no light would dare touch my face for fear
of what it would highlight.
Ripples of my being have only just settled,
have only just come to rest on the edge.
The days were extended, it seemed all had ended,
so I just don't want to talk about it.

Never As Good As It Seems

I speak, and it is searched . . .
the tone monitored . . .
the reason questioned.
The colour of the shirt I wear is wrote about,
The choice of colour apparently leads to some
hidden sexual orientation . . .
Apparently . . .
If I close my curtains I am hiding . . . if I
leave them open I am flaunting my wealth to the world.
Constantly the subject of microscopic probing . . .
Just because they see me every now and then, why is it
they feel they own me? Who stole the deeds to my life?
I didn't sign my rights away that very day when the light was
shone my timid way . . . what happened to *my* say?
With the flip of a coin goes their following . . .
One side, fresh from the mint, with its seductive new tint,
the embodiment of the dream . . .
The other side, the worn and blunt, the litter's runt . . .
Like the novelty, has lost its gleam . . .
'It's never as good as it seems . . . '

Love Is Such A Viscous Thing

It's rotting. I don't know why, but it is -
The shock to find that death lays inside,
Quite literally. A lump of stone, cracked for some time.
No use or purpose, serving only as a constant reminder.
Red droplet stains are all that's left - where once great rivers ran.
When you took your axe and cut me deep from sharpened tongue,
I had no way to stop the flow,
So slowly died.
From red it drained of all its colour,
And now is split, an idle block.
As blade to throat of sacrifice -
Or stone to frosted glass, that's how it was!
You scarred me, a scar that even I can't see,
But still I feel.
And how it felt? . . . As if inside you were let loose,
Swinging axe to all you set your eyes.
And now abandoned, a disregarded wreck, you cast me out -
You set me sail to oceans to remain.
Forever present, yet not, the soul has gone -
And all remains is an ever floating shell.
Until it sinks, as did my love, in my heart's blood.
Love is such a viscous thing.

Offering To You

Am I wrong, to be afraid?
When my world is crashing down.
All around me, the sound of bomb like explosions,
If I were a cliff, I would be taped off,
due to extensive erosion.
I do not know the cause,
everything just seems so wrong,
so out of place, and all my problems,
so 'in your face'.
I feel like a broken record,
turning with such intent,
yet getting nowhere, all because
against it leant the hindrance of a scratch.
Yes, one tiny scratch, it seems no match
for the human mind, humanities spine,
but looks can be deceiving, it's the little
things that matter most,
the tiny and intriguing.
Now, caught in the spin, amid cycle,
amid the wash, I am stripped of myself,
Cleansed of my qualities.
I am no longer what I thought,
I'm becoming what the world sees.
Just like me to try and please,
each and every person with a view.
I murder myself,
As an offering to you.

Your Brand

It hurts, when your reality is put on hold,
your channel muted. Simply overlooked.
When every breath that you give life
is near always mis-took.
People see you in a light, that's very rarely right,
is very rarely true at all, but still that's what they see.
You call to them, in subtle ways, increasing with your pain,
'Attention seeker' they declare, but there is nothing for you to gain.
Self butchery you turn to, separating flesh,
creating new scars daily, there's not much surface left.
Of course when people ask you, excuses spring to mind,
'I cut my wrist there yesterday, whilst fiddling with the blinds'.
When alone at nights, in the darkness of your room,
with one lone candle burning slightly by the wall.
The a-z of scars that travel from your elbow to your hand,
shine timidly as your trademark, your description and your brand.

I Read You

The introduction, a smile, a friendly handshake,
Oh what a lasting impression, I'm sure that will make.
Chapter one, edging in, slowly but surely.
The character description, history and traits.
The plot begins to fit its mould,
Two pages stuck . . .
The surface cold.
But remembering, I'm only one chapter done,
I cannot judge, when hardly begun.
As chapters turn to thirds,
And the pages flow like water from a tap,
Overlooking my own prejudice -
I slowly filled the gap, between good and bad,
I looked beyond your cover,
And saw what lay beneath.
I read you for the book you are,
The opposite to my prediction.
I glanced upon your surface quickly,
But missed your true inscription.

Robert McGarry

I was born 4/6/56 in a little farm house with no toilet or running water, in a place called Kilmahamogue, beside a bog in Ireland. I moved to the local town when I was 4 years old and pretty well lived there ever since. Due to the Cold-War I had a mental breakdown, which led me into the realms of the mad for 20 years, where I spent most of my waking hours trying to achieve peace on earth through prayer and telepathy. This meant I had little time for my personal life or interests and could not care for myself. The lasting delusion caused by the breakdown left me feeling personally responsible for all deaths occurring due to wars between 21st September 1982 and 21st September 2002. Throughout this time, all I thought about was reasoning out possible solutions to the conflicts of the world. Luckily I only swore my life to this task for 20 years when naked and crazy in the isolation room of the local mental hospital. Since September 21st 2002, I have reintroduced myself to my local community by running in a local council by-election and chairing the Moyle Music Collective. I also write songs as may be seen from my rhyming verse. The reason for all my troubles was, I believe, caring too much and thinking all people are equally capable of understanding the simple truth, no matter what level of intelligence:

Think, speak and do only good, 'We get what we give.'

Listen To Me

I am the law giver and I say unto you
Stop this fighting let's start anew
There's just no excuse it's against the law
To kill or be killed like a lottery draw.

When you meet someone new just let it be
Religions invisible why bother to see
My nation's the world, to it I belong
No politics of hate let's all sing along.

Most people are good and the bad are troubled
The will of God, their self-conscience gets muddled
Never fulfilled always feeling doubt
Yet without opposition what do politicians shout?

Now I believe in majority will
Let all the world vote 'cause it's not long until
We'll all be connected by technology
Yes or no, it's as clear as night and day.

I Object

It's been a long time since man declared war
On everyone else who didn't agree
And now they don't know the why and what for
Soon there'll be no enemy to see.

We're not alone in believing, it's a fact
There's peace on this earth accept for the few
With them I'll definitely not make a pact
It's obvious they're worried, anxious and blue.

It's easy to grasp, it seems that most know
Keep us informed it's the best for all
Don't declare war to distract with a show
We know what you're up to, making weapons we will fall.

Ask the world's people what's right and what's wrong
They will decide and if all are honest
Before the bell tolls and we hear the last dong
Cry out for peace and make it your longest.

I'll Pay The Fee

I think I know the why and when
It's up to us be sure to count to ten
Ten seconds are up, time to decide
And remember this, there's nowhere to hide,

You're on the spot, make up your mind
Be sure that what you decide is kind
I'll feed the starving, the world clean up
We've got to get out this silly rut.

We have the means to do it now
For long enough we've milked the cow
We can't clone a new earth, then move over there
This couldn't be done, we'll just have to care.

Calm

When will peace-time happen?
When will the swords be sheathed?
Our strength is sapping
Because of human belief.

It's easy to talk and then depart
You'd never know just what you start
So stay in contact, don't give up
Remember you drink from the truthful cup.

It's all so mesmerising when there is plenty
All in hope that the prophet sent may
Forgive them all for worshipping greed
And leaving many in poverty and need.

We know how it works for we are the builders
But it's taking over, soon nothing to sell, dears
Only food for the belly and warmth in the hearth
Will have any value, for what it is worth.

The life that's so precious
On the earth for sure
Won't act on just guesses
No money could lure.

Out there, there are many who know what I mean
Acting in unison their work's unseen
Struggling hard in the name of good
Surely soon it will be understood.

Join In

It's funny but there was only one star in the sky
The decision was mine whether to live or die
So all the others who live inside
Soon found out there was nowhere to hide.

They helped the light of life in its work
And what they got back was more than a perk
They felt the earth give out a sigh
Something dwelled in them, 'I believe' was the cry.

Then the heavens lit up with stars in their millions
Created by faith in ourselves, we're no minions
And now that we share more than we dispute
The future looks good and it's a promising route.

We'll end the wars and feed the starving
And hope there'll be a lot more caring
A time will come, Utopia's birth
When reason will rule on our beautiful earth.

I'm with you in mind
And know you are kind
So I hope you soon find
Some way out of the bind.

Revealing

What is this alien being I know?
That seems to be the author of the show
Maybe it's something from way in the future
Making its presence felt like a massive computer.

Never sleeping as time through us flows
Back to the stars the enthusiasm grows
And maybe if we paid heed to the notions
To better things, we would guide our motions.

For the better good avoiding conflict
Always knowing when to be strict
And if the doors for you are opened
A note on a postcard, to me send.

What yet to enter the realms of mind
Surely on this world more of my kind
And may life decide peace on earth
An end to worry, just enough mirth.

Takes Time

The sands of time are running low
It'll soon be time to reveal the show
Not yet my friends many aren't ready
For now just keep your pressure steady.

When, oh master of all that's right
Will those who believe have enough might?
When leaders elevate to a higher level
And cast aside the works of the devil.

It's happening now all over the world
The computer, information, to millions hurled
Ones with money who can afford such things
Control over the big discussions it brings.

I know there's many starving, it's true
Peace on earth should bring justice to the few
And when the machines of war are carrying food
The devil defeated, only good.

The Beat Of The Earth

Pow! Pow! Pow!
The beat of the earth
I love this place, that gave life birth
I care so much, it's like I know
I'm the only one who really knows life's show.

Man carved its surface to suit his will
Yet it fights back by nature's shrills
It seems the poison will soon it smother
If those who know don't start to bother.

We can use greed to support the struggle
Make it more profitable to clean things up and not juggle
At the end of the day it's no more than a promise
This chance, we can't miss.

Justice

Look down from your position earned through life
Remember you're a man, you can stop the trouble and strife
All you have to do is judge humanity as one
Trying every angle even the Father and the Son.

If you see the good in man and give him greater powers
Please don't allow the capital to be wasted on corporate towers
And if the one whose grace redeems allows us further years
We'll bless them with more happiness, less shedding of sad tears.

So peace come now, not yet fully shown
Soon to many it will be known
How to advance into future time
And create a little jovial rhyme.

Level

I think by now we've reached a level
Where we can discharge the works of the devil.
Who's right or wrong won't need a decision
It will be totally obvious due to derision.
We'll learn to obey the general will
Somehow we'll agree and our hearts will fill
With understanding of minority views
Never in a position to win or lose
But care we must for all around
Make love and peace for all abound
Politicians the world over will see the sense
Get off the fence
For nature's defence.

Capture The Conscience Of All The Earth

I'm a human being, of that I'm proud
Yet the being part is shouting loud
You poison the air, river and sea
And your fellow human you can't let be
But wait a minute, that's not me
I'd like everybody to believe they are free
End the wars then you'll see.

A time to care, hold out a hand
If you love life don't pollute the land
And maybe all will then be fed
For it something's ain't done soon we'll all be dead
Forget about your daily bread
Many have said
Where's that led?

So if we don't get hit by a comet
Or from drinking too much, choke on vomit
This new year coming will be the next step
Towards peace on earth, I'd like to bet
But yet
It isn't set
The being part is still wet
And can't be trapped in a net.

Capture the conscience on all the earth
Envelop it before it gives birth
It's happening now please understand
As is written, at whose command.

Openness

Hello everybody, in the world
It's a night to live, not get bored
All the banners shall be furled
The dove of peace, to the heavens soared.

Imaginations all set free
Hoping things will come to be
Maybe a prayer from those who believe
No longer the masses, the few can deceive.

Only big secrets now exist
Your particulars probably on a computer disk
Scanned and looked upon as a list
Losing the content can be a risk.

Say out loud only words that matter
This will cut down on useless chatter
Then only the big secrets will be discussed
And I hope any outcome will be just,
A must!

An Answer

The threat so great the power was given
To save all life before it was driven
To extinction by the folly of man
Funny thing was my mind said I can.

If you can reason out just why
Our leaders sometimes seem to want to die
Or maybe they don't know what they do
Enlighten them let them start anew.

Now with a fresh start and understanding
With love in their hearts they'll start commanding
The things required to save us all
So the precarious hold we have won't fall.

For hunger and death await us there
For tomorrow's dawn we have to care
We can't command the sun to rise
All we can do is listen to the wise.

The solutions for me are already in mind
Yet it seems that many are still blind
Enough thinking done it's time to act
I don't want to perish and that's a fact.

We learn we decide but change comes slow
Why it's this way I just don't know
To speed things up should be our task
Reveal your inner self remove the mask.

We are no longer actors on a stage
If we are it's time to turn the page
The play is written and that's a fact
Altogether now in the final pact.

Care for others like you love yourself

Forget the honours, praise and wealth
No one's alone we rely on each other
Don't serve greed it's not your mother
You can't eat money and I'll take it further.

We're connected you know for we share this Earth
I ask you to speak out give common-sense a new birth
I believe for what it's worth
That together we can give hope a new birth.

Communicate Gently

I love the world - and everything in it
To another world - there's no way I'd flit
But I gotta say - and say it out loud
That I don't think somehow - humanity can be proud.

We've poisoned the air, we've poisoned the water
We consume energy like it doesn't matter
And far off somewhere in a foreign land
There's a fellow man needs a helping hand.

So let's live for the day we all can feel happy
Let's have no sad faces, no tongues that are ratty
And if we get on with one and another
There'll be no bother.

Brenda Turner

I was born in Fenton, Stoke-on-Trent, Staffordshire and brought up along with my sister. I was first of all in Abbey Hulton, Stoke-on-Trent, but do not remember much of this, as I was only four-years-old and my sister was six.

When Dad changed his job and went to work for the railway as a porter, we moved to Leekbrook, near Leek in Staffordshire. My most treasured memories as a child are in that small village. My other sister was born there, who is eleven years younger than I.

From 1966 I was working as a medical receptionist, really enjoying this interesting work and meeting so many different characters until retiring at the age of 60.

My hobbies, writing poetry and stories, began in 1964. Photography is another of my interests. I have always been fond of outdoor pursuits and nature which give me my inspiration to write poems and stories, all of which are true and authentic, things I have experienced during my lifetime, nature being the recurrent theme. The reason it is so interesting to me is because I enjoy putting all my thoughts into focus, keeping my mind very active.

Looking back in time and recalling pleasant memories of years gone by, there are many lessons to learn in life and we can benefit from them - I have.

Photography, also inspired by nature, animals, scenery, mountain ranges, beautiful sunsets, the sunrise and waterfalls, all part of my inspiration. Self-motivated. This makes me feel I have achieved something good in my life.

The camera is my constant companion and together we capture some wonderful wonders of nature.

Our Four Different Seasons

S uch a lovely vista once the *spring* is here,
P rimroses, daffodils, wild flowers and memories dear.
R are it is you ever see the cowslip flower today,
I n the countryside they were never far away.
N ot as many bluebell woods we would always see,
G one are the days when most wild flowers always used to be.

S pring is fading now, but *summer* takes its place,
U nder the ground new flowers waiting to show their face.
M aybe in a little while the earth will show these flowers,
M any, if not all of us, given lots of happy hours.
E njoyed as well, the fruit that always comes our way,
R ed cherries, raspberries and vegetables, these crops are here to stay.

A ll the seasons, especially *autumn* always do appeal,
U nder all the colours, trees, they now to us reveal.
T inted gold, red, orange and brown, yellow, all-aglow,
U nderfoot the leaves we kick up as we go.
M uch pleasure we all have from this, whether girl or boy,
N umerous changes with each season, things that bring us joy.

W aiting now, the *winter*, very cold but you can see,
I nteresting birds, especially the robin sitting by the tree.
N ever has his little breast changed so bright a hue,
T hanks to nature these pleasures are enjoyed by me and you.
E ver admired a snowman, built with so much pride,
R emembering the fun you had as a little child.

Changing Seasons

The green leaves are falling; the birds change their song,
The summer it seems was not very long.
Its warmth and beauty seem so far away,
It gives way to cold air, unwelcome each day.

First it rains and then the leaves start to fall,
Before long we know autumn will call.
Some parts of autumn can sometimes be bright,
Leaves changing colour, a wonderful sight.

Before we know it, winter is here,
Cold days and long nights, very lonely I fear,
But winter has a beauty of its own you see,
As the snow falls on hedgerow, plant and tree.

We scrape the icy window when we first get out of bed,
The spider has been busy, spinning a silky thread,
We see it in the hedgerow shining bright at dawn,
Little birds walk in the snow, leaving footprints on the lawn.

As the snow falls quietly to our Mother Earth,
Keeping it, oh so warm, for the newest birth
Of the snowdrops, the crocus and other plants too,
Bringing joy to everyone which includes me and you.

Before we know it, spring is once again here,
New lambs and foals, also baby deer.
The fox and her cubs venture out of the den,
The circle of life begins over again.

Warm days, short nights, now we know why,
The summer sun has returned to the sky.
All the earth has awakened from sleep,
And again breathes in, the summer heat, deep.

For all creation there are many reasons
Why we have this change in all of the seasons.

The Wonders Of Nature

What do you want out of life, may I ask,
Is it wealth, riches or power?
Chasing these three, an arduous task,
But just think on a bright early hour.

Animals and birds care for their young,
Most truly a wonderful sight,
Praises to them, many times I have sung,
How quiet they become through the night.

The sound of dawn chorus, I would never exchange
For all wealth, riches and power,
These three, will always be out of my range,
But what of a cool summer shower?

The earth is refreshed; shoots start to appear,
Many different, we see every day,
These are the treasures I love to be near,
When I listen and learn nature's way.

Summer, autumn, winter and spring,
All change with the passing of time,
Each season it's very own beauty will bring,
The enjoyment of which can be mine.

So, what do you want out of life, may I ask,
Is it wealth, riches or power?
The wonders of nature do these far surpass,
Each moment, each day and each hour.

Our Changeable Weather

In the garden one Sunday afternoon
So peaceful and quiet, not even a tune
From the birds today, so very still,
Usually with birdsong, the air they would fill.

The weather is clammy, no sun, but so hot
Even without the sun, cannot find a cool spot,
Grass is so yellow, brown and so dry,
Need a downpour of rain, not a cloud in the sky.

Then the hot sun came out, but a breeze stirred the air
Where before, a really hot atmosphere had been there.
That's better, much cooler, a gentle touch,
A cool breeze that was, appreciated so much.

But the weather is so changeable, now, a sunny day,
Too hot is not pleasant for me I must say.
But wait! Hot weather at present has passed,
At 16.09 rain for the garden, at last.

Thunder rolls round the heavens, a comforting sound,
It brings heavy rain, soaking the ground
Which will be so refreshed after the shower,
In such a short time, 16.20 the hour.

What of the birds? Must be having a rest,
Tomorrow at dawn they will be at their best,
Dawn chorus to wake us up, a new day,
There's a lot we can learn from Mother Nature's way.

A Day At The Brecon Beacons

One day we went to the Brecon Beacons, in winter, it was very cold,
Wild scenery like this always beckons; open space for miles will unfold.

There was a man climbing the fall, so cold it had frozen you see,
The father to his son would call, 'Buckle up,' concerned he would be.

Safety precautions were in place, we watched, he continued to climb,
Quite slowly at a steady pace, what a change in so short a time.

It was summer when we went there before, the waterfalls running free flow,
In this season it seems you open a door, such beauty and wildness to go.

Must be the call of the wild, the adventurous self, deep inside,
Treasured thoughts I always had as a child, in a place of adventure to hide.

Pen-Y-Fan is such a beautiful place, peace and quiet, there is no fear,
Variety of seasons with a different face, free running streams, crystal clear.

Time is taken up with so many fears; true friendship seems to be gone,
So sad, the changes over the years, when life could be so much fun.

There was my daughter, surveying the scene, Yasmin, faithful friend
by her side,
One of the most beautiful places I've ever been, vistas so spacious
and wild.

Now we are on our way home, after a fun-filled day,
Everyone said with a solemn tone, 'Wish we were here to stay.'

But we had a good day at Pen-Y-Fan, fond memories of that day,
To go there again we will have to plan, and it is not so far away.

Mountains And Valleys

Over the mountains and down in the valleys
We meandered along by the banks of a stream,
Hand in hand through the bluebells and shadows
Nature's wonders could clearly be seen.

Mountains and valleys make up our memories
Woodlands and rivers varieties of flowers,
Which we had shared so long ago
But now they will never be ours.

My mind goes back to those happy times,
A world of our own where we wanted to stay,
Memories there, I will always treasure,
Never made that new life on the way.

A Beautiful Day At The Park

This beautiful place we saw as we walked
On a day I was spending with you,
The day really hot as we strolled and talked
The lawns freshly cut and new.

Look, a squirrel running down the tree,
I thought he was cheeky and brash,
Seemed very tame whilst running free,
We were close, but he'd gone in a flash.

Came across a waterfall, tranquil and cool
The shrubs were guarding its way,
It flowed into quite a large pool,
We were enjoying the hot sunny day.

The boating lake seemed like fun,
People enjoy the whole scene,
I would encourage all to come
To this park, the best I have ever been.

As we meandered we heard the band
Playing tunes from a favourite show,
Phantom of the Opera, on the open stand,
Listened, then on our way we would go.

We were admiring all the flowers
A really beautiful sight,
In this park one can spend many hours
In summer, when everything's bright.

Imagine the view from the side of the lake,
The gardeners can be proud of this,
Wandering around, all the time you can take,
Spending hours, so full of bliss.

The band played very well we must say,
Enjoyed the musical break,
Among other things, this made our day,
Pleasant memories back home to take.

We found a pleasant place in the shade
After enjoying a wonderful day,
Those memories of ours will not easily fade,
The sun kept the blues away.

My Sister And Friend

E very time I am distressed and feeling rather sad,
U nderstanding you will be, someone to make me glad.
N ever have we quarrelled, on you I can depend,
 I will always think of you, as my special friend.
C oncern we both have, this I know, and have to say,
E ven when unhappy yourself, you never turn away.

M ine and your sadness will soon disappear forever,
Y our kind words and thoughts, help me to endeavour.

S o dear sister Eunice, if the time you find,
 I n your very busy life, just keep me in mind.
S ome time in the future, please come stay with me,
T wo or three days will do, you surely then will see,
E very time you come to visit, a thank you I will send,
R emembering you will always be, my sister and my friend.

Meditation

Meditating on freedom of birds on the wing,
To them life is good, they have everything.
Except and agree, I'm sure that you must,
In mankind they haven't a great deal of trust.

Just take a step near and away they will fly
You will then see them soaring way up in the sky.
When winter approaches, away they will go,
To some warmer country without any snow.

No hustle or bustle, no rush to and fro,
No waiting for trains or buses and so,
Ahead of them lies a new lease of life,
Away from the hazards, frustration and strife.

If it were possible, and I'm sure you know why,
With those happy creatures would be you and I.

The Jaguar Automatic

Now here is a story I am going to tell,
As it happened things turned out quite well.
My friend arrived in her new *Jag,*
Brought along a picnic bag.

First time in it for her you see,
Listen to this, a poem by me.
Try as she might, couldn't find gears,
Amazing I said, she's been driving for years.

Trouble is, never driven it before,
Watched with interest as she opened the door.
You see this *Cat* is a *Jaguar* automatic,
That's why she had problems, very erratic.

After deciding to go down to the sea,
The performance we had as she turned the key.
Tried to go *up* a one-way street *down,*
Good thing we were not in the middle of town.

Can you imagine this interesting scene?
In a new Jaguar, feel like a queen.
Don't forget this was my friend's idea,
As she tried once again to put the car into gear.

Remember to wave to the crowd, my friend said,
They all waved back then bowed the head.
Who is this dignitary coming our way?
Imagine their thoughts on this beautiful day.

They cannot see who it is until we are near,
Someone quite posh! Up goes a cheer.
They will be disappointed you will see
When they realise, it is only my friend and me.

We now decide not to go too far,
My friend is concerned about parking the car.
I wonder where next we would go,
It's a dangerous road, she said with great woe.

Well driving along, still very erratic,
Trying to control the *Jag automatic.*
Now we try to find a good place,
To have lunch, as she drives at a far faster pace.

At last we park up, glad that is done,
Photo call finished what a great run.
Hope the photographs turn out well,
They always have a story to tell.

Although it took all day we agree,
My friend is used to her car now you see.
Driving much better, not so erratic,
A day of adventure, in the *Jag automatic.*

Our Fun Day At Tesco

This morning I rang my daughter, are you going shopping today?
Call and take me with you, she said, will be there without delay.
She hadn't had her breakfast so I made some toast and tea,
We were in a hurry, an appointment I had you see.
Have to be there by eleven, will we be home by then?
Sure we will, my daughter replied, although it was nearly ten.
We locked the front door, went to the car, we didn't have a care,
Depending on how long it takes, we may have time to spare.
Arrived at Tesco, collected our trolleys, shopping had begun,
Weather was good, sunny and bright, be glad when this task is done.
Hurried and scurried round the store, trying to save on time,
All is well up to now, everything seems fine.
At last we had finished buying our food, trolleys full to the top,
Quite a good stock of provisions, from our favourite shop.
We now stand waiting in the queue, ready to pay our bill,
I was finished, my daughter, not quite, but near the end at the till.
Disaster strikes, my daughter finds she doesn't have her purse,
How much is it? I will pay, but things are about to get worse (£99)
Assistant swiped my bankcard to take the money out,
Sorry, not enough money in she said, of this there is no doubt.
Dear me, what can we do, now to put things right,
Such an embarrassment for us both, can you imagine our plight?
A second smiling assistant appears and wonders what can we do,
I said, 'Put it in cold storage, we will come back to you.'
'Very well then,' she said, 'that can be done I am sure,'
'Only until we have the money,' I said as we walked through the door.
My daughter is very honest as I am, you all will see,
My daughter responded, this is my mother who will say anything for me.
My daughter's purse is back at work, but the journey's short,
To go and collect the money for the food we have bought.
So if you come shopping with my daughter and me, life will not be a bore,
Just come with us to Tesco, our very favourite store.

Mariana Zavati Gardner

Mariana Zavati Gardner was born in Bacau, Romania on 20th January 1952, the daughter of Artillery Colonel(r) Constantin Zavati, a chemistry teacher and Iulia Bucur Zavati, a pharmacist.

She studied at Vasile Alescsandri Boarding College for Girls and passed the Baccalauréat with distinction.

She specialised in languages at Alexandru Ioan Cuza University of Iasi and graduated at Master of Science in Philology, double first class honours.

She did a postgraduate course in Education at the University of Leeds and postgraduate courses at Goethe Institut Rosenheim and Ecole Normale Superiéure Auxerre.

She is a member of The American Romanian Academy of Arts and Science USA, LiterArt XXI The International Association of Romanian Writers and associated member of the Poetry Book Society.

These poems are about the need to care for the environment, the need to share one's life with young and old and the bond that exists between people and animals.

In our political world, one needs to stop, listen and hear the deep and beautiful sounds of our planet.

These poems are the answer to various emotional experiences and a personal way to deal with change.

Confused?

This morning some people forgot to get up
Some people missed their train
Because of anxious weather
Some forgot tea arrangements
Because of tiredness and dizziness
Or a tactful last minute headache
Doubts would justify other people's
Dry mouth, loss of appetite or sickness
They can now grasp the meaning
Of clear ringing in their ears
Passionate doubtful disputes
Are in progress over boundaries
Moving words makes one feel sweaty
Capricious or unsettled for weakness
It's common, it's normal, it's passionate
Time does not improve one's condition
So many people have no voices
During the day many people forget to wake up

The `Lies´ Display

Every year, during carnival days,
Crowds join in politicians
Who are knocking glitzy bells
Of all sorts . . . of all sizes . . .
Who are breaking steam
Politically decided as correct;
During various meetings,
Where only one person emerges
To ring the shining bells of surprises,
Irresistible lies are displayed like a dream
Fascination in the battle of words
Fictional boats in the stream of thoughts
Unaccountable thrilling excuses
Reflected smash and grab explanations . . .
Politicians must always be correct!
Every year, during carnival days . . .

Spinning

Past into the future
Horses standing still
In the exhibition of equestrian art
I track the tired pages
Of new catalogues and brands
Free addresses of magic spin
Retailers of dreams
Moving world of fancy dress
Gondolas on infested canals
Petrified cries
In moving carriages
In rolling on coaches
Last summer racing horses
Were available in the pages
Of new catalogues and brands

A Sea Of Too Many Thoughts

It has been raining just sand
Here and there a pebble or two
Stony breathe on slimy ice
People one only guesses exist
Are hiding in various houses
Of various prices, of various sizes
They live the life of an island
Surrounded by water that touches
Low and high shores and feast
With the hungry seasons
Now and again these people get ready
To leap into a sort of black holes
When the time is thought to be right
Prim and proper tides surprised
Run away beyond a sea of too many thoughts

Route 66

Layers of melting speed
Rolling on and on
In the deep-frozen heat
Bikers caught in a trap
Flocks and flocks
More confusion delayed
Running together
For a different meeting
Storming distant bees
Cars with the old plates
Zooming ghost trucks
Harassed autumn wasps
Soul of bikes most of past times
Arise along the old Route 66
Standing some furious speed

The Flute

The Indian flute my daughter is playing
In the small room the size of a cage
Was bought from a faraway place
This passed summer in the scorching heat
Trapped is she by her feelings and the hard work
Many days lie ahead with toils unaccounted
The youth has no time to be young . . .
She is turning old every day with the rain
Weather forecasts tell of the hours
She could have done something else
My daughter is playing the Indian flute
My son is crushed with emotion
The summer has passed . . . we are turning to winter . . .

Summer Visit

Our summer visit was in the mountains
The desert was coughing with dust
The sun was biting and creaking the light
The mid-afternoon was preparing to die
Above the Music Mountain lizards
And cacti were fighting for spaces
Like caged grasshoppers were singing
The sky was burning an oven display
The spaces of stone were all around
Much stone and sand to spare and no water
Displays of turquoise beads were on view
And sand pictures from legends
About some people who vanished
And left their thoughts behind
Some in stone, some under the soil
Red from the iron ore for all to see
And maybe feel their souls wandering
By at Little Big Horn and beyond
It was as if we have never been there . . .

Alone On A Day Of Summer

Arching beauty of the sun at noon
Sheltered garden mirrored in dry pond
The court of love has been postponed
Today will stay . . . would never dawn
Tomorrow left alone to clinical details
A house, a shed with scorching roof at noon
Under the apple tree with wooden swing
The wheel of fortune likes a game of chess
The lovesick souls might choose to chant
Before the scorching breeze takes over
Of secret pilgrimages subdued in shadows
Departed house with apple trees and swing
The weary road of time . . . waxed canopy
A journey ended on a day of summer

Beyond This Universe

It was getting dark in the close with many closes
The street with so many cats and a number of dogs
The street with singing bushes and a pepper of trees
There lived the golden hamster with the fur like a fox
The magical old hamster that came there with the fall
The mind of a mirror in the old battered soul locked
And opened in shiny, glittery laughs, always smart
A gentleman of those very old schools, so much
Forgotten at present, on purpose . . . he travelled . . .
He travelled this world, twice with the neighbours . . .
Gently Thanksgiving arrived . . . the old magical soul . . .
Was floating the direction unknown deep at night

It was getting dark in the close with so many closes
The street with so many cats and a number of dogs
The street with singing bushes and a pepper of trees
The magical old hamster that came there with the fall
The golden hamster with the fur like a fox was gone

Mornings

Letters arrive at my door early
Every day except on Sundays;

Rain grips chanting terracotta roofs
Silence sets in every street and alley;

Milk comes with lead showers
Every day except on Sundays;

Days . . . nights . . . all merry-go-round . . .
Seasons allow each one to remember

Too Soon

That rocking horse
Made of wood
This rocking horse
Made of plaster
That baby's rattle
Made of silver
This baby's rattle
Made of plastic
The music box
Made in the mountains
My son played with
Before he went to school
He had watched the music
Made by showers on windows
Same teddy bears
The frog with yellow eyes
The silent puppet otter
Mobiles humming in the air
Light reflecting other toys
In the attic my young husband
Boarded at half term one autumn
Too soon the age is moving on . . .
The showers and the seasons . . .

A Storm In The Soul

It was dark . . . lights in conversations
The old man was getting older
People were standing indifferent
To the slow fast passage of time
The egg timer was in view silent
On the window sill next to the sink
The old man was washing up
The old man was getting older
Still home sick for the buffalo hunt
A storm in the soul of the winter
Voices from the forests
With roaming grizzly bears
Voices from the prairies
Oceans apart and medicine men
Counting the plates and the glasses
Setting the forks and the knives
And the spoons in the right order
Waiting for the holy midnight
The old man was getting older

The Family Tree:
Constantin Bucur's Birthday

It came via the post one morning
It was early spring . . . my uncle was eighty

Time to look again at the family tree
On thin sugary paper and blue fountain pen

Some people I knew
Some people looked of no particular age
Some people had no clear or sharp faces
Some people I might have met
If I were older . . .
If I lived somewhere else . . .
It came via the post one morning
It was early spring . . . my uncle was eighty
Still like the fresh spring at heart
A cavalry man he had been . . . brave . . . wounded
In the last tragic war, memories in an album . . .
Less loud and elusive . . . leaves in the air . . .

Displaced in another world, I often recall
These people who made me what I am
The seasons rolled like a dream
The albums . . . the family tree . . .

Never Ever

Vagrant images in albums
Cures for incorrigible travellers

In time, at stations, on platforms
Dreams would flow slower

Expedient trees with crying leaves
Are the dividing memories of summer

James Cameron

Having been born in 1954, in a rural market town in Lutterworth in Leicestershire, I attended Junior High School and Lutterworth Grammar School where I excelled mostly in art, drawing and painting, which I still do.

I joined Her Majesty's Royal Navy as a able-seaman (Tas rate) anti-submarine warfare operator for an 8 year stay aboard HMS Tiger for three years, travelling to Gibraltar, Malta, the Persian Gulf, Iran, and other gulf states, during the Vietnam conflict in the 1970's. From there I joined HMS Hydra, a survey vessel, for an 18 month stay, which was one of the best times of my life, visiting the Seychelles in the Indian Ocean and surveying all of her many beautiful islands. My last posting was at HMS Victory which is in Portsmouth, being a guide on Nelson's flagship for an 18 month stay, where I excelled in history of the Napoleonic period. In 1979 I joined the merchant navy, serving aboard a super tanker for 6 months, taking on oil from the Persian Gulf states. From there I joined a supply boat for 3 years working mainly out in the North Sea, taking out food, clothing, fresh water and fuel etc to the North Sea oil platforms, which was dangerous and exciting, while being based at Montrose and Aberdeen. From there I joined another supply boat out in West Africa, based in Gabon, for a year, which was the most dangerous place that I have ever witnessed, where life is cheap, and death is common place.

Having seen the world, I left the merchant navy and came home for good to work alongside my family in their retail business for 2 years in Northampton. In 1993 I came to the Isle of Man, where I started to explore many exciting possibilities, using the talents that I possessed - writing novels, poetry, prose, fairy tales, illustrating, graphic design and inventions, which are all still on-going. I have several fairy tale stories and a personal collection of 600 poems which have not yet been published. I find my inspiration comes from being alone, surrounded by nature where one can positively think in quietude. Where often I listen to classical music, such as Mozart, Haydn, Handle and many more exciting composers whom inspire one's spirit to achieve high levels of enthusiasm in attaining my goals etc.

My hobbies and interests are reading history, poetry, non-fiction, the great classics of yesteryear, such as Lord Byron, Mary Shelley, Percy Bysshe Shelley, Keats and many more great poets. Writing children's fables, reading philosophy, collecting books and antiques and oil paintings, drawings etc.

The Poor Souls Of The Earth

The poor souls of the earth, whom are needy,
And when someone genuinely is discovered,
We can all do something constructive and positive for them,
All the poor souls of the earth, may know that love has been given,

When that good Samaritan came busying along,
With his kind, generous nature that was shiny like gold,
To help his fellow brethren who had fallen victim, and old,
From lack of care, when society turned its back on him,

Who once gave his life in service to his country,
In both world wars, he was miserable and cold,
But he survived for a reason, so he could help others,
Whom are less fortunate than others, who have never been rich.

To witness all the poor souls of the earth, whom are hungry,
Where in Africa, India and South America, it usually means from birth,
Little children, who have no hope or shelter,
Having seen their parents cursed, with no bread and water,

Where they starve to death in skin and bone,
Where life is cheap, and the bullet is strong,
Where the gunman came running along,
With bombs and grenades, he shoots willingly,

Believing in revenge, and that one day he'll reach Heaven,
But how wrong he is, when he deceives his own country fellow men,
With no arms, the baby cries her painful death,
Where punishment is the golden rule,

For all orphans, with no mother and father,
Where the family unit is disintegrated in tears,
With hatred's banner of suffering, and her fears,
Mockingly, as the young soldier smiles at the defeated one.

All the poor souls of the earth,
Where disease is champion still,
As the rocket grenade came thundering on,
Where the landmine took both his legs away.

The poor souls of the earth, whom are needy,
And when someone genuinely is discovered,
We can all do something constructive and positive for them,
All the poor souls of the earth, may know that love has been given,

Where daily existence is like a tragedy and nightmare,
To brave the streets of crime ridden cities alone,
Scavenging for rotten and decaying food,
In the gutter, the warlord wickedly smiled at the unfortunate one.

The poor souls of the earth, whom are needy,
And when someone genuinely is discovered,
We can all do something constructive and positive for them,
All the poor souls of the earth, may know that love has been given.

The Rose Lady

Inspirational, where madame writes her memoirs and letters,
Whilst listening to sublime music, of yesteryears' musicians,
Serene, graceful and inspirational,
With o'ertures of beauty strong, indefatigable and consuming.

Where the rose lady walks across the landed gallery,
With the sweetest perfume wafting in the atmosphere,
So sad, so lonely and macabre, her tired spirit trapped in the ether,
Forever, lost in another world in the eighteenth century grieving.

Doomed to live with no convenience, where the spirit cries,
Of love and romancing in the summertime gardens,
O where is thy love on the paradise landscape,
Where we used to walk reading fine poetry, muse and art.

Together arm in arm, underneath the latticework of red roses,
With Greek and Roman classical busts on plinth and column,
Besides the lake and pools, the sunshine ripples,
As the rose lady walks the estates in deep mourning.

Invisible and ghostly, she appears and reappears,
To find her love has gone forever, under the green weeping willows,
Across a bridge and mown lawns, a black carriage appears,
Bringing melancholy thoughts, where plates of fog disappear.

Where stag and deer dart, jumping so clever,
Where once Madame walked in a bright new world,
Viewing the estates with love and pleasure,
As all the lark and songbirds loose their feather.

Where autumn comes, shedding leaves of orange-gold,
Upon a carpet of bluebells that cover the forest floor,
Where the wind is slow, labouring and whispering,
As Madame opens up her umbrella of gold.

So enchanting and beguiling, sequestered and remote,
The white winged horse flies the nightmare skies,
Where moonbeams shine pleasantly down,
Accommodating Madame's ghost leisurely underneath the maple leaf.

A million thoughts flood my mind of her disposition,
Once a spirit that roamed freely, enjoying life and love,
Where it is written in her secret diary, her love that died,
Oh pleasure, oh pleasure has gone forever.

Compelling as it was with fury and disappointments,
With blast and wind, blowing furiously,
Across the bleak moors, I saw your spirit crying,
Just calling me, for the want of nothing but love.

Oh Augustus, be quiet and peaceful,
Where your guardian angel is waiting,
To take you to paradise and heaven,
Inside the arms of love, I shall adore you for evermore.

Inspirational, where madame writes her memoirs and letters,
Whilst listening to sublime music, of yesteryears' musicians,
Serene, graceful and inspirational,
With o'ertures of beauty strong, indefatigable and consuming.

.

Aimlessly Thinking

And if it were not for me, aimlessly thinking,
I would shudder aimlessly by a tree,
Which is fully grown in the early mist and dawn,
Whilst aimlessly thinking, why I confess at all.

As I gazed lovingly at a fair woman of such sweet beauty,
Upon a sedate orange leafy green lawn,
As far as the eyes could see, a brightened picture,
Where her wooden swing went to and fro.

With better days, I touched my breast,
And felt a murmur, oh yes! A frightful murmur,
That was forsaking me, a terrible love was dying,
It was forsaking me, underneath the bluest skies above.

As sweet Augustus smiled, a thousand thoughts with her two lips,
Which were quiet and closed, with her shy repose,
With her youth so delicately exposed, and wanting,
Whilst finding love without depressions, and blessings.

To hear, to see, to feel love's hope and tragedies,
Is a heavenly sweet sent blessing from far above,
And if it were not for me, aimlessly thinking,
I would know of no worldly pleasure at all.

Than to see a goddess of muse with all her remarkable treasure,
With the summertime flowers scenting on the wind,
With all nature feeding incredibly, and prolifically,
With a vassal of love which finally conquers all,

Sedately, in the forest and woods, offering up a prayer,
I search no more of beauty's intricacies,
Where water nymphs splash delicately around,
Diluting the five senses remarkably well to beauty's sound,

Whilst aimlessly thinking of love,
Of what only love can do, superseding,
Is to bring you its final wise lesson,
Aimlessly thinking of what you should do.

And if it were not for me, aimlessly thinking,
I would submit myself freely to love,
Where a nightingale sits singing sweetly above,
Essential, exploring freedom on liberty's far-flung wing,

To be with you my fair sweetheart, and friend,
Calling and wooing as one, disposed to love,
With reason, philosophy, and wisdom,
Where the reflection is true and good, with endurance,

I would not of made that final decision to simply die,
Within the shadow of my sweet love sighing,
Where beauty was unbelievably strong,
I knew then my heart was broken wide,

Underneath those heavenly universal glittering stars,
Paramount with a longing love letter,
That never arrives, in the snow drenched morning,
I plead with a supplication towards heaven.

And if it were not for me, aimlessly thinking,
I would shudder aimlessly by a tree,
Which is fully grown in the early mist and dawn,
Whilst aimlessly thinking, why I confess at all.

A Special Place

Across England's mighty blue seas,
There is a magical place,
A beautiful island covered in yellow gorse,
Many times I have been to this place,
It's a special land,
Where dragons are slain,
Where dreams are made,
It's full of enchantment to take your breath away,
Where you can go back in time,
To find your inner peace,
Where orchestras play brilliant, inspiring music,
The music will blow your mind,
Where it remains in the soul,
Where boys grow into men,
Where kings are made,
Where love is found,
Where pretty ladies dance all year round,
True romance lingers the sweet air,
Where fairies remain,
The wishing well of time,
The Isle of Man,
There's no place like it to be found.
In mid-Atlantic stream,
There is a special kind of kingdom,
A beautiful island, where Vikings once stood,
With battles of long ago,
Now but whispers on the wind,
Celtic legends, mythical of a romantic kind,
Where knights and princes have fought this land,
Down the centuries, a web of golden secrets,
Ne'er to be told, but only a king will know,
The wisdom of his exile,
The beauty of the Man.

O Mozart, O Mozart

For all who sing his name,
We all sing in classical overtures,
O Mozart, O Mozart, O Mozart,
We cherish thee in a beautiful part of history,
The eighteenth century, O God gave you wondrous talents,
So special, so wonderful, so very pleasurable,
He has risen to greater works, our hero Mozart,
Now he rests with his beloved wife, O Constanze,
O be glory to them, a prince of powerful inspiring music.

The world has known great men, great statesmen,
But of music, this fine, inspiring gentleman,
O Mozart, O Mozart, O Mozart,
Who composed with feeling, with emotion,
With enthusiasm, with heightened creativity,
His great works in prolific abundance,
With style and grace, in the period of renaissance,
Where rainbows shine down upon the earth,
Where sweet couples courted, where they romanced.

In grand eloquent song, the noble genius that he was,
Sublime, courageous, the triumphant sound,
To the serenade of a violin,
Where he played the harpsichord aloud,
Where the orchestra play in virtues,
Where the pianist plays Mozart, O Mozart,
Bring in the power of the clarinet,
For he reigns in supremacy, every night,
For he moves in the world with supreme vibrations of light.

On A Leicestershire Highway

What world are you from Madame,
Surely it is from a bright worldly universe,
Where only the heavenly stars shine down in glory,
Where beautiful words are sang in verse.

Thy Venus child so vivacious and gay,
In brightest fields of gaiety and laughter,
Filled with spontaneity on a glorious day,
In a world of love, romance and thunder.

Let temptation be no man's pain and curse,
While the English highway remains invincible,
Where brave memories receive your courtly smile,
On this road to a thousand journeys and miles.

Let no one keep those joys apart,
In longing days so genteel, and bright,
Always with plenty smiles, pleasure and delight,
Here upon this Leicestershire highway.

Where extravagance is the ruin of many men,
Where love only speaks its kindest words,
In bravery, benevolence, and duration,
Where no provocation lays claim therein.

This wild fiery passionate realm,
Where only etiquette and politeness remain in,
What would the French say, beaux ideal,
That of excellence, and enchantment, inside you feel.

When the child of Venus brings you red roses,
To place around your waist, a band of glittered poises,
She even blows the stars down to thy heart,
Placing in your hands brightest red rubies of the night.

Wrapped in your winter cape, so beguiling,
The midsummer eve sparkles with every diamond,
Where treacherous men have fought and died,
We ride black horses, on a Leicestershire highway,

And I have seen tempestuous women proud,
With the fury of denial, enriched with heaven's pearls,
With despair of loving you triumphantly,
Oh come Madame, show me inside your heart,

A world quite different from hell itself,
Where I have watched you with sentiment,
O loving you, with celestial complexities,
Whilst dreaming of Utopia's magic and excitement.

Illuminating the classical gardens, with colour,
With every variety of roses and clematis,
Nature's fury comes with bolts of lightning,
With awe and magical murmurs, pertaining to beauty.

Tis, a wondrous moment of expectation,
Whilst walking with history and observation,
Arm in arm with an English poet, just daydreaming,
While Madame muses with her correspondence and letters,

Amongst unseen spirits, who vanish with virtues,
That are tremendously attainable within the secret garden,
Are multitudes of sumptuous wonders,
Making one feel idyllically peaceful and blessed.

With expressions of greatness and privilege,
Unequivocal, demonstrating Madame's fascinating world,
Without revolt or discriminations spoiling,
Our investment of passionate ploys.

Oh Jupiter and Mars, with invincibility,
At night-time, we see the tempest stars,
Promising and promoting joyous hours,
Where victory is seen in your reflection.

What world are you from Madame,
Surely it is from a bright worldly universe,
Where only the heavenly stars shine down in glory,
Where beautiful words are sang in verse.

Freda Grieve

Born in Glasgow, Scotland and now, since her husband's retirement, lives in Formby, Merseyside. Formby began as a Viking village and is now a safe home for the red squirrel in the Freshfield Nature Reserve. Freda Grieve enjoys working with a theatre group back stage and with an embroidery group. A member of the Association of Christian Writers and the Society of Woman Writers and Journalists. She has three young grandchildren to help her with market research. She is mainly interested in writing poetry and stories for children.

'Work is influenced by the things I feel most deeply about and also my life and family. Ambition to follow my dream of enjoying writing to the utmost'.

Several poems published in magazines and anthologies and some success with short stories and articles. This year taken a home study course on writing on the Internet with Lancaster University.

Has two books of short stories for children published in the USA this year. Print on demand books.

Stories to set good examples to young children from the age of three up with an interesting books. Reading for themselves or having them read as bedtime story by an adult.

Believable situations and dilemmas of every day life with believable outcomes. A touch of fantasy woven into the pages to hold the interest of the very young reader to be.

It would be wonderful to collect 15 to 20 poems together in one book for interest to my grandchildren and that's why I'm submitting poems with themes of interest to children.

From The Dark Side Of The Moon

Children gather near, this is a tale most terrible to hear.

In the days when the world was new
There grew a monster of gigantic size
With fierce and bright and burning eyes.

A dragon from the dark side of the moon
Landed in Sockburn and took over the River Tees.

This devouring beast did exactly as he pleased
Drank and swam in milk from cows, in an enormous trough

And if that was not plenty, for country folk to bear
There was not a soul brave enough to dare
To ride the land of the Sockburn Worm.

Till the Lord of the Manor
Turned to folklore of the land
And found that help was at hand,

In ancient tales of the Tees Valley,
Old men had written on worn pages, of the Sockburn sword
Planted in a stone in the village square
Left to be forgotten truth to tell.

Well, when everyone got such a fright, the Lord of the Manor
Drew this magic sword, and cut the worm in a million pieces
They all swam down the River Tees and vanished from sight.

What Am I?

I am love
I am joy
I am the laughter
Along life's way.

I am April
A storm of tears
Quickly played out
To be replaced
By a watery smile
Sunshine after rain

Tiny scrap, battling to survive
Growing stronger day by day
So much to learn
So much to say and do
The present and future
Lead me on.
The world is a journey of discovery.

Wise Advice

In the land of Jungle Green
It is best to look and not be seen
By Lion, Tiger and slippery Snake.
Try not to make a sound
Tread softly on the ground,
And whisper when you talk.
Above all don't run,
Just walk.

If you see a Crocodile smile
While taking a mud bath,
Don't laugh and stay around
Believing that you have found
The perfect snap,
A holiday winner.
Still as a log of scaly wood
He sits posing looking good.
One wicked eye half-closing
Taking a nap in the river.
This big-toothed grinner
Is dreaming about dinner.

An Explorer And His Dog

You call my brown dog Pooh Bear
And he must look big to you,
For the world is an adventure playground
When you are only two.
Soft loose snow, drifting deep on the lawn,
Making an Antarctic wasteland since early dawn.
Paw pad and Wellington boot sink deep,
As you drag a sledge and he makes a leap
To bound ahead.
Snow on the shed like an igloo's icy roof,
His woof is sharp with the thrill of excitement.
By its tone I can tell he has dug up a bone,
But for you it is a pirate's hidden treasure.
It gives me pleasure.
To watch you there,
With the dog you've re-named Pooh Bear.

Swinging And Free-Wheeling On His Wheels

Cheery faces of class three,
Helping hands put up the tree,
Running feet to tie each gift,
In brightly coloured wrapping.
Stop! their teacher cries,
Treetop touches ceiling.
Must snip, bit, for pet free-wheeling.
And class made the best tree yet.
Saving choice titbits from lunch
Took great care with decoration.
And wished him 'Happy Christmas'.
Later the bunch thought the hamster very rude,
Even chewed the tree, along with all his food.

Frog

Funny frog
Sits on a log

What if the wacky fellow spoke
Would he tell you of his day?
The way he likes to jump and swim
And how all fishes look up to him
Seeking words of wisdom and advice.

Wouldn't it be nice
If the frog when he spoke
Was a comedian with a joke
Dancing on long, spindly legs
Perfect to prance on dry land
Or flipper flap in the river.
This giver of laughter and glee
Would finish with a witty ditty
And sweep a bow to you and me.

What a pity
The frog when he spoke
Did nothing better
Than croak, croak, croak.

Almost One Of The Family

The moment the car
Turned into the road,
She went to visit a friend.
To me it was the end.
The final straw.
After all, he was almost
One of the family.
And you have to play host
Or in our case hostess
To a guest.

It was bad enough
Before Christmas
That sharp exchange
Beside the tree.
Sister shot upstairs
Refusing to come down for tea,
And he sat with an inscrutable look
Till the family took their leave.
I could not believe
Her persistent disdain.
I've pointed out again and again,
You have to get on with relations.
She replied with a toss of her head
'Cousins perhaps, but dog and cat
Were not meant to be friends
And that's that!'

How Bottle Hill Got Its Name

Once upon a time a farmer was forced to sell his only cow
His heart was heavy as they struggled up the steep hill to the Fair
Then out of thin air stood a strange little man blocking the way
Wrinkled face, pointed sharp nose and red eyes of a goblin
Wrapped around in a great coat although the day was hot
'I'll pay for your cow with a valuable bottle'
The farmer should not have agreed to such a foolish bargain
'It will deliver you from all your troubles'
The seed of greed was sown and the bottle exchanged for the cow
'Go home and get the table set. Put the bottle down and call
Bottle do your duty'
The farmer's wife had a good mind to throw the thing away
'But,' said his little girl, 'the bottle has magic powers'
'And it's ours to try,' said his little boy spreading a clean cloth
'Bottle do your duty,' the farmer gave the magic command
And two tall servants of the bottle brought fine food to the table
On gold and silver dishes more than they were able to eat at one go
'You exchanged our cow for a fortune,' his wife's vow became a smile
They sold the gold and silver plates and became rich
The cruel landlord was paid his rent
Long before the good fortune was all spent
But he got to hear about the bottle in the Market Square
And putting on a friendly face promised to be fair
'Bring the bottle for me to see and you could own the farm and land'
'Bottle do your duty.' No sooner had the farmer put the bottle
On the landlord's table, than a flash of light and two servants
Jumped out chasing the landlord all about the room with wooden clubs
'Get them away and take your bottle back. Keep the farm forever'
And whenever the farmer and his family talked about that day
They all laughed and cheered remembering the goblin on the hill
'The bottle has delivered us from all our troubles.'

Dad

He listens and understands
For he was once a boy.
Mends a toy,
Reads a story,
And teaches
All the family to swim.

Because of him
They walk tall
And learn.

This man with wheels
That drive away
Each day.

Is king of the road
To his kids.

Young Busy Mum

Busy Mum
On the school run
Taking three to classes.

Primetime passes
Picking up scattered toys
Searching out football gear
For boys.

Standing on the sidelines
To cheer.
Trying not to shiver
In the bitter cold.

You don't have to be old
To receive a bouquet
On Mother's Day
Just the one
That's special.

Dickensian Day

People came out to play their part
In the art of creating a day gone by,
Lace trimmed bonnets and tall top hats
Beadle, town crier and boy in flat cap.
Girl in frilled apron and long skirt frock,
Joined crowds who flocked round stalls.
Books, bric-a-brac and lucky tombola,
Roll a dice, land on number, for a prize.
Eyes turned to Morris dancers' skill
Till Punch and Judy show began.
Bell rings rang out good cheer.
Summer is packed away for the year.
But Christmas puts warmth in the heart.

Letter Poem To My Grandsons

You came on a visit for my birthday
I watched you walking tall, almost nine
And thought of the time that summer
When you were eighteen months old,
With toy watering can, getting splashed
As you helped to tend the flowers
In your garden back home.
Be a gnome with magic rain
I tried to explain the power within.
Imagination like a magician's wand
Weaving a special spell.

You never fell for that
But lead me gently to the kitchen tap
Where I meekly filled your can
You stood by with a childish grin
Till water reached the very brim.

Your brother now just looked at him.
A six-year-old going adventuring.
With wooden sword and shield
'There's an awful lot of dragons
Around Grandma.
An awful lot of dragons in your garden,'
He said with a determined stare.
Waving his sword in the air as he
Chased an imaginary pair up a tree.

I do not know what you both will be
When you reach the age of men.
The future is not mine to see
But these glimpses make me smile.

Humming Cloud

(Poem by my eldest grandson Stefan Grieve age 10)

I look into the sky
High in the sky
And there, oh why
Floating on high
A fluffy cream cloud
Humming aloud
To the soft country beat
So you can tap your feet
To the slow cloudy beat

Such a tiny thing
This singing thing
With its whistling hoot
It can toot along
To a lovely tune
Under the moon

This fluffy ball
Is giving a puff
To a lovely lullaby

As I look on high
I wonder how, why?
This thing as a gift
To hiss a cheerful tune
Of wonder and joy?
Oh boy!
Time for tea!
Oh lucky me!
As I went inside
I looked up on high
And whistled joyfully

Mark Stead

Mark Stead was born August 28, 1973 in South Africa. His early childhood was filled with a love affair for poetry, which he started to produce from an early age. His initial poems expressed his desire to understand the world around him, which he found aloof and unyielding. Finding love for the first time, his works took to expressing the emotions associated with new relationships - both the kindling and the extinguishing of love. Writing throughout High School, he went on to study Finance at the University of Cape Town. After completing his degree, he followed it up with a post-graduate qualification.

Following three years working in Cape Town, he decided to move to Paris. It was here that his work took yet another turn. His arrival in a foreign city and exposure to a language he had yet to master presented new challenges and provoked new comments on the immersion into new worlds and new adventures. From dark tales of misplacement to the excitement of the unknown. From the unforgiving nature of fate to the exposure to another culture, his poems have rippled over the recurring themes of 'why' and 'for what cause', interspersed with the longing for his home-land and the discovery of love to the anguish of heartbreak and betrayal.

In addition to writing poetry, Mark has also completed a, as yet unpublished novel, The Shadow Game. A thriller involving a hidden code, a mysterious syndicate bent on destroying the European monetary system and with it modern life in Europe for their own gain and a group of three individuals who know about the plan and are willing to die to stop it.

He is a passionate reader of all genres and enjoys travelling the world in search of exotic locations and stories. In addition to his first novel, he has also started a follow-up work entitled The Rathlin Conspiracy. A thriller that takes the reader on a chase from the Second World War and the discovery of another element more powerful than uranium, back to the modern day and the real reason behind England's continued possession of Northern Ireland.

As well as the thriller genre he is working on a literary comical novel about the misadventures of an eleven year old boy as he plots to kill his parents, trying out his crazy schemes on his cat, Samson and his dog, Gabriel. He has also written a number of short stories.

He currently lives in Paris, where he works full-time in amongst his writing.

Will You Be All Of This?

Will you be my guide?
Will you hold my hand
and will you walk beside me?

When I falter will you aide me?
When I fall will you help me up
and when I move too slowly will you encourage me?

Will you be my water?
Will you be my sunshine
and will you be my shelter against the rain?

When I sleep will you wake me?
When I tire will you put me to bed
and when I cry will you comfort me?

Will you be my torch
as I stumble through the darkness of life
and will you lead the way?

Will you be my sunrise,
my dawn and my dusk
and will you be my sunset?

Will you support me when I triumph?
Will you revel in my successes
and will you cry in my failures?

If you will be my life
I will be yours
and if you give of totality
I will surrender completely.

I will be all that you give and tenfold more
I will be all that you dream of
and all that you wish for.

But I will only be all of this
If you are all with me
For you are the one that completes my world.

A New Beginning

The morning sun steps graciously out
leading in the new day
the rebirth and reawakening
the revitalising of a cold and darkened soul

a long deep sleep
light enough to understand
deep enough not to care
the lifting of a shroud

the revelation of living
after an undignified death
the spark of passions
the lightning of dreams

waterfalls of colours
erupting onto blank pages
creating movement and spirit
re-energising a tired mind

a gust of happiness
after a long silent depression
a pierce into the darkness
the stirring of unimagined greatness

the sense and smell of anticipation
alive inside a hollow core
stretching out to fill the void
replacing nothing with everything

discarded thoughts remembered
lost wishes returned
untainted smiles
and unlearned hopes

tangible life
unassuming
unexplainable
revelling in the ecstasy

a new day
a new life
a new birth
a new beginning.

Naked

My hand shivers above you
Naked, you are like the morning mists
Your body curves, changing pathways
Your skin, golden like a desert sunset
I want to breath in your beauty.

To devour you with my eyes
Your soft lips, moist, ripe peaches
The lines, tender over your stomach
My fingers slide toward you.
Naked you are like a silver moon
Defiant in the night, alive in the darkness
Your eyes bright, holding me tight
As I cautiously move, over you

I take you like a hunter
All of you, breathless beneath me
Rising up to meet my body
Naked, you are the world itself

5 Minutes To Midnight

Out the window
the black world awaits
its dirty hands roam everywhere
lose direction and its fingers shall lead you astray
the quiet outside
so silent, so unknowing.

Shut up tight in this warm world away
so peaceful, so safe
separated from the outside by a thin piece of glass
and as the clock moves along
the morning approaches
and once more the safe little room
will be left behind as is ventured into the outside

But do not worry as return shall come
and back to this place shall step
and once more the clock shall read the same time
and once more the morning shall approach
and once more,
and once more . . .

A Feeling

A feeling buried deep
never heard
never expressed
kept hidden
never left free

there exists a moment
a single moment in time
where all else stills and becomes silent
and all that remains is the feeling
a suppressed feeling
so far covered
so long forgotten
and in that crack in time
that feeling becomes too great to bear
it erupts through
enveloping everything
what it touches
is left changed
something different; better,
better in a way that few can claim as known

the emotion so great
that words do not its power tell
a start, an end

linked in a circle of time
never to stop
but to run forever
till all that is left
is the feeling
and life becomes that feeling
so powerful
a power beyond this and the next

a green light on a white wall
a purple shower on a blackened floor.

A Better Life

Oh friend,
why doth thou look so glum?
And why sit you so crouched in this cold and lonely place
These blank, endless walls shut out the world
so come, let us leave this dreary abode
and make haste for a better land

A home under the sun
where we can walk down gold-cobbled pathways
and live magnificent stories under blue candle trees.
We can bathe in crystal clear lakes
and breathe the life around us
Our sight can span the horizon
with nere a wall to block it short
We can run like the rivers
and jump up to the stars

So come with me now
and let us go
for the sun and moon shall not hesitate
they shall 'ere continue
until all this around us is gone
and we are but memories lost in time
Let us live our lives now
lest soon they be gone.

Our Little Place

As life slips through our fingers
silently unnoticed
we undertake our journeys
that stretch toward a final ending

and somewhere tucked away
in that jumble of thoughts and messages
of images so clear and those forgotten
we realise this plight
and try to ignore it

everyone has a place to go
a place that however insignificant
makes you forget the outside
forget about what lies ahead
and what lay behind

and makes you remember
that what really counts is the day
not the week or the year
but the time we have now,
and we so want to believe it

and as time drifts along
like a feather on a breeze
so shall we continue
until all that is left is
what was there before,
nothing.

Solutions To Our Holocaust

Life is no longer a joyous occasion
In this black world
to be born not a blessing
but a curse

to grow up in this sewer of death and misery
is a burden not wished on the blackest of hearts

we are not all brothers
but mortal enemies
protecting what little we have
and trying to take that from those

The power of life
like a dwindling candle stands
ready to forever disappear

and we all move blinded
by our own hate and distrust of those around

we would rather kill than talk
And oh how wonderful it is to take life
For surely in this world
a world which we by our own means have created
is not fit for us to inhabit

The time has long passed
For us to look inward at ourselves
for it is there that the solution to our holocaust exists

Touch

Touch not what is there
but instead reach over
and touch a little deeper
a little further away

to that which you cannot see

speak not of what you know
speak of things unknown
remember places never been to
and faces never seen

laugh at stories never heard
and cry of sadness never felt
stretch out to that beyond

and you will reach that, that is unseen
but touch that, that is always there

I Will No Longer

I will no longer bow down to passion
no longer hail love
no longer cherish friendship
but instead shall live a life
that is untainted
untainted by emotions and thoughts
and I will die a lonely person
with all but myself to hold me
and nothing
not even a footprint in dust
shall I leave behind

What I Love

I love the morning sun
    rising steadily in the cold night air
I love the sea, the waves
    and their endless intrigue
I love the cool breeze
    that sneaks across on a hot day
I love the mountains
    that stand so dominant
I love the noises of the city
    and the quiet of the country
But above all this
    I love you

This World Of Ours

(An address to travellers)

Welcome to our world
where we exist in the makings of our own inhumanities;
we are the lovers of death;
    the patrons of destruction;
    and the poets of the apocalypse.

We live in this place of futile beginnings and glorious ends,
because we do so love it.
So take heed all you travellers of note;
This place you enter is not of which you are used.
It is unlike anything you have experienced;
It is a playground of war and of evil,
It is a cage from within which you'll never escape.
And beware you innocent souls,
Beware that by chance,
you might actually enjoy yourselves!

Taking life is unlike anything;
It is, in itself, an art form.
It is the pure expression of one's dark side.
That part of us we all ignore,
    and perhaps forget.
That raging beast that sleeps so baby-like inside,
    Until it is awakened -
    then the fury that erupts is enough to
    frighten the devil himself.

For in us all exists this dark might
but heaven forbid it ever gets out,
For then who are we to predict how it might act
and who are we to try to control it -
    for surely it is not us

Ah, but it is us,
It is us when we are born,
and it is us when we die.
It is us in times of trouble
and it is us when we are threatened.

So don't ignore it,
Embrace it and use its strength.
For the weak don't survive;
they merely get erased by the strongest.

Long live this world of ours!

Josephine Ann Easterlow

Let me introduce myself. My name is Josephine Ann Easterlow. I live in a village called Tur Langton, five miles from Market Harborough, but I was born in a small Leicestershire village called Thurmaston on November 30th 1945, under the star sign of Sagittarius.

As far back as I can remember I have had a fertile imagination and the ability to draw, paint or to write it down in the form of short stories and poems. The only thing I didn't have enough of, was time.

I married at eighteen and by the time I reached the ripe old age of twenty-three, I had five children to look after, (I grew up with my children.) It was only when they flew the nest did I find a little time for my writing and as my grandchildren came along (14 plus two great at the last count) it was them that took interest and encouraged me in my art and writing.

Six years ago my husband bought me a computer, this opened up a whole new world for me. I found inspiration and a wider audience for art and literature.

Jim Morrison once wrote, 'real poetry doesn't say anything, it just ticks off the possibilities'.

I have to agree with him, it opens all doors and lets you walk through any one you choose. When I'm writing I live within my words. My love for dolphins and Stonehenge is echoed in a lot of my poems. I have many interests in life but most of them revolve around art in some for or other. I have a portrait of Jim Morrison tattooed on my back along with dolphin designs all my own artwork.

Well I think I've said enough now, I hope you will enjoy reading my poems as you walk through my kaleidoscope of emotions only I, lady of dreams, will know the true meaning that lies behind each and every one . . .

The Blue Rose

The world was white covered in snow;
the blue moon cast a silvery glow,
Everywhere glistened and shone real bright,
there was magic and mystery in the air tonight
The stars were like diamonds, shiny and new,
I held my breath as I took in the view . . .
I was not alone as I stood by the tree,
I could feel his dark eyes watching me,
As he stepped out the shadows he held in his hand
a perfect blue rose from a far distant land.
My heart quickened, for I knew it was he,
who had brought this rare blue rose to me.
And so with the mystery and magic of the night,
I took the blue rose and my heart took flight.
My spirit was captured, my soul on fire,
not even the cold snow could quench my desire.
Our spirits entwined, infused with love,
as little blue rose petals fell from above.
Then just as we were to be one,
the clouds hide the moon the magic was gone.
But I still held the rose with its colour of blue
and I know one day . . . I'll find the way
and give to back to you

Summer Of Fun

A vast radiant beach, music from the caves
Laughter all around, dreams in the waves
Cool jewelled moon on soft, damp skin
Open up your mind, let imagination begin
Eat from my table, drink the wine of love
Reach forth touching the tender prize above
We glide to the sea, bath in freedom's beach
Music floats around the moons within our reach
Vibrant memories scattered in the sun
On a radiant beach in a summer of fun

Messages

'Remember me', the message simply read
It started thoughts inside my head.
I remember the laughter, the fun at the start
I remember the passion as you captured my heart
Then I remembered the tears, the pain
No . . . I'll not travel that road again
So I tapped on my keyboard without further ado
And messaged him back
How the hell could I forget you!

A Golden Bird

A golden bird flew into my world today
Tired and weary, it had come a long way
It started rainbows dancing in my head
It glittered and shone as it lay on my bed
It brought from you
A message of peace and love
Thank you my Lord for my golden dove

The Cry Of The Dolphins

As I watched and listened to the sea
Something stirred deep inside of me.
I didn't know what, I didn't know why,
But I knew I could hear the dolphins cry.
I was thinking of what the news flash said,
Ship in trouble, man overboard - feared dead!
The sea was rough, waves thrashing around,
The tide brought in a loud eerie sound.
The moon's silver light shone over the sea,
I could still hear the dolphins calling to me.
What was the matter? What was wrong?
The rain was falling, the wind was strong.
Then I saw them jump up high into the night,
Casting a shadow in the moon's silver light.
As I dived in the sea I was feeling real calm,
I had nothing to fear, I would come to no harm.
As I swam nearer, I could now understand more,
They were trying to bring his body up onto the shore.
They had brought him in with caring heart,
Now on my own I must play my part.
I dragged his body onto the beach,
Out of the ocean away from her reach.
Things happened quickly, help came to hand,
My part was over; he was safe on dry land.
I waved to the dolphins as I turned to walk away,
Then a voice rang out and I heard it say,
'Thank you for saving this off-spring of mine,'
I'll remember you till the end of time.
'For saving your son,' she said as she looked out to sea,
'Thank the cry of the dolphins, don't thank me!'

Dream Lord

As lady of dreams I entered your world.
I swam in on a wave of blue,
Dream lord I told you to believe in me
And I'd believe in you.
You shared your dreams with me,
You opened up your heart,
Only to find I pulled you down,
And kept us worlds apart.

Dream lord you believed in me
With a heart that was so true!
But this lady of your dreams
Still could not believe in you.
Slowly but surely she started to thaw,
At last dream lord she opened the door.
Feelings ran high, the pleasure, the fun

But *oh* dream lord look what you've done!
Did you mean to break her heart?
Is that what you set out to do?
To enter the land of the lady of dreams,
And tear it in two!

From her you stole the sparkle
And took away the sun.
Well done my lord of dreams!
I guess that you have won!

To Dreamlord from the LadyOfDreams.

Memories In The Sky

Did you see the moon tonight shining in the midnight sky?
It brought back so many memories, it reminded me of you and I.
As the sun sank in the west we were always miles apart,
Yet so very close locked in each other's heart.
Did you see the stars tonight, twinkling way up high?
It brought back many memories; it made me want to cry.
I will love you till the stars fall from the sky, is that not what you said?
And how I had to see a star before I'd go to bed.
When I was lonely and feeling blue, I'd look at the sky and think of you,
You would say did you see the sunset tonight?
I was thinking of you when I took in the sight
And I too would be doing the same,
Looking, just whispering your name.
But now when I look up into the sky,
I think of you and just ask why?
Why did we drift apart? Tell me what went wrong?
How did you break the link . . . that I thought so strong?
Questions with no answers . . . feelings pass with time . . .
But I will always remember . . .
When I was yours . . . and you were mine.

From Dolphin to Dr Seuss

Help Me

I'm trapped, I cannot breathe, I'm struggling for air,
I need a lifeline, someone to help, someone to care.
I'm cold, I'm frozen; there is ice in my veins,
My memories are fading, only heartache remains.
I am losing all the fight that's inside of me,
I am no longer mistress of my own destiny.
Then out of the blue in my torment and despair,
Your thoughts reached out to show you were there.
Just when I thought it was over, that this was the end,
I heard the voice of my soul mate, the keeper, my friend.
Slowly but surely I started to thaw,
You turned the key, you opened the door.
You showed me the way down 'Moonlight Drive',
I am smiling, I'm warming, and I know I'll survive!

From one soulmate to another.

The Calm Of The Dolphin

When life is too much and it's getting you down,
When you feel like you're swimming and you're going to drown,
Sit down and think of a wonderful place,
Shut out the bustle, the rush and the haste.
Put away the frown and wear a smile,
And feel the calm of the dolphin, just for a while.

When I am down and feeling low,
I have a place in my head that I go.
Where the sand is white and warm to the touch,
Where the sea is cool and inviting so much.
As the waves rush in to touch the shore,
I feel the calm of the dolphin once more.

I walk to the water slowly with care,
To find the dolphins are waiting there.
I take on their form, and follow with ease,
I swim and I dive and I go with the breeze.
I'm weightless, I'm floating, and I'm starting to glide,
I'm happy, I'm swimming and I'm riding the tide.
I'm ducking and diving, I'm under the sea,
The calm of the dolphins is inside of me.

Time Before

Skylark soars high into the midsummer sky
Waiting to hear her hawk's love cry.
A spirit of joy and love flying free,
High over the mountains, over the sea.
Then coming down to relax and rest,
In the village back in time that she loved best.
Time before bloodstain this land,
Time before white man made his demand.
Time when you could hear the leaves of spring,
Time when you could hear an insect sing.
Time when nature ruled this land,
Time before white man made his demand.

Another love of my life, The Native Americans

Wind Chime Memories
(To my husband with love)

One Christmas I'll always remember
It started to snow that night in December
Everywhere was wrapped in a blanket of white
As we walked hand in hand in the bright midnight
The moon shone down, we were happy and free
As you hung up my wind chime for the world to see
Snowflakes were falling like butterflies out of the sky
The trees were frosted with diamonds that caught my eye
The haze of the moon with its ghostly beams
Cast a light of silver on my frozen dreams
Christmases come and Christmases go
But I'll never forget that night in the snow
The chimes are still there hanging rusty and old
Their sound still brings in warmth from out of the cold
Their tune brings back memories of sweet delight
As I smile and I remember that Christmas night

The Prisoner

(We are prisoners of our own device)

Looking out my window onto a field of dreams
Where the butterfly sings and dragonfly screams
A coloured caravan and a gypsy fire
Wake up my dreams, rekindle my desire
Look through the window of my soul, look into my eyes
Tell me what you see there, tell me no lies
That's one window I will not look, I wouldn't dare
For your memories and secrets are deeply hidden there
Out into the fragrant air the adventure's here it seems
Rambling fields, curling smoke and twisting little streams
A vast, radiant beach and a cool, jewelled moon
I heard his voice call me way back in my room
I closed my eyes and turned to the wall
And when I looked back I saw nothing at all
I closed my eyes as I heard him say
Enough now!
Look through your window some other day

SpotLight Poets

I'm Lost

I've tried and tried but I've tried in vain,
I've laughed and I've cried in the winter's rain,
I've tried. But tell me what can I do?
Something is baring my vision, blocking my view.
I've tried to pluck dreams from out of mid air,
But the inspiration has gone, it's just not there!
I need to reach out for something anew,
I need some excitement from out of the blue.
I need to jump onto a dragonfly's back,
I need the inspiration the words that I lack.
I need to see fantasies and dreams once more,
I need the ice inside me to thaw . . .
I don't want tot be someone I'm not,
But I am it seems!
I want back my imagination I want back
The LadyOfDreams!

Goodbye My Friend

I had a phone call yesterday
To tell me a young friend had past away
Shocked but not surprised
I wiped the tears from my eyes
Brain's on the brink, can't take no more
Afraid to open his eyes
Afraid to open his door
Emotions all mixed up, feeling all collide
Debts and drugs wrapped in confusion
He's on the downward slide
He cried for help and reached out but no one wants to know
He's took as much as he can take, no place else left to go
And so in desperation he took his life in hand
Alone and in the darkness he past through to the promise land
I picture you all tears in your eyes
For a young guy you all knew, but didn't heed his cries
Me . . . ? I'll just smile and say . . .
Goodbye my friend, I hope you find
A far better world than the one you left behind

A Kiss

A kiss frozen in time
A kiss yours and mine
A kiss waiting to begin
A kiss from deep within
A kiss that will mean so much
A kiss waiting to feel our touch
A kiss that will make a seal
A kiss that will make us real
A kiss frozen in time
A kiss that tells you I am yours
    And you are mine

Imagination's Dream

As I slipped into my lonely bed,
I closed my eyes real tight
So many thoughts inside my head.
It was hard to leave you there tonight
And then as if by magic,
I was standing in a yard -
With a magnificent view,
Two arms slowly encased me,
These arms belonged to you.
I was in a yard where the roses bloom,
And the mountains reach to the skies.
I leaned my head against your chest,
And looked into your eyes.
I folded my hands around yours
As they clasped around my waist,
Two dreamers locked together,
Two hearts . . . just one pace.

The Lizard King

*(This poem I left on Jim Morrison's grave in Paris
along with the portrait I drew of him)*

Lizard king with your insect eyes
Poison venom . . . sweet surprise
Wrap your roots around my soul,
   Feel me, eat me, take control,
      Come taste my passion. Open my door,
      Enter my world and heart once more.